FORTY-THREE
SEPTEMBERS

Also by the author

The Gilda Stories
Flamingoes and Bears

FORTY-THREE SEPTEMBERS

Essays by
Jewelle Gomez

Firebrand
Books

Earlier versions of these essays have appeared in the following period-
icals and books: *Between Ourselves; Breakthrough; Bridges; Essence; Les-
bians in Midlife* (Spinsters Ink); *My Father's Daughter* (Crossing Press);
Reading Black, Reading Feminist (New American Library); *Sing, Heavenly
Muse; Ten/Eight; Testimonies* (Alyson Publications); *Trivia; Wild Women
Don't Wear No Blues* (Doubleday).

Book design by Betsy Bayley
Cover design by Lee Tackett
Typesetting by Bets Ltd.

Printed in the United States on acid-free paper by McNaughton & Gunn

Library of Congress Cataloging-in-Publication Data

Gomez, Jewelle, 1948–
    Forty-three Septembers : essays / by Jewelle Gomez.
      p.   cm.
    ISBN 1-56341-038-9. — ISBN 1-56341-037-0 (paper)
    1. Gomez, Jewelle, 1948–   .   2. Afro-American women authors—20th
century—Biography.   3. Authors, Indian—20th century—Biography.
4. Lesbians—United States—Biography.   5. Afro-American lesbians-
-Biography.   6. Fantastic fiction—Authorship.   I. Title.
PS3557.04577465   1993
814'.54—dc20   93-34681
                                                        CIP

Acknowledgments

My grateful thanks go to the many who've helped shape the ideas and words over the months and years: Dorothy Allison, Nancy Bereano, Elly Bulkin, Cheryl Clarke, and Linda Nelson. And to Eric Ashworth, Marj Plumb, Colin Robinson, Brenda K. Brown, Michael Albano, Nellie McKay, Val Wilmer, my family in Boston, Pawtucket, Erieville, and now San Francisco. And to my prince, Diane Sabin.

As always, my work is dedicated to
Gracias Archelina Sportsman Morandus,
Lydia Mae Morandus, Duke Gomes.

Contents

I LOST IT AT THE MOVIES

Me with (l-r) my grandmother, Lydia, great-grandmother, Grace,
and mother, Dolores (1949)

My grandmother, Lydia, and my mother, Dolores, were both talking to me from their bathroom stalls in the Times Square movie theatre. I was washing the popcorn butter from my hands at the sink and didn't think it at all odd. The people in my family are always talking; conversation is a life force in our world. My great-grandmother, Grace, would narrate her life story from 7:00 A.M. until we went to bed at night. The only breaks were when we were reading, or the reverential periods when we sat looking out of our tenement windows observing the neighborhood—whose sights we naturally talked about later.

9

So it was not odd that Lydia and Dolores were talking non-stop from their stalls, oblivious to everyone except the three of us. I hadn't expected it to happen there. I hadn't really expected an "it" to happen at all. To be a lesbian is part of who I am, like being left-handed. It seemed a fact that needed no articulation. My first encounter with the word *bulldagger* was not charged with emotional conflict. When I was a teenager in the 1960s, my grandmother told me a story about a particular building in our Boston neighborhood that had gone to seed. She described the building's glorious past through the experience of a party she'd attended there twenty years before. The best part of the evening had been a woman she'd met and danced with.

Lydia had been a professional dancer and singer on the Black theatre circuit: to dance with women was part of who she was. They danced at the party, then the woman walked her home and asked her out. I heard the delicacy of my grandmother's search for the right words, even in the retelling. She'd explained to the bulldagger, as she called her, that she liked her fine but was more interested in men. As she spoke I was struck with how careful my grandmother had been to make it clear to that woman (and, in effect, to me) that there was no offense taken in her attentions, that she just didn't "go that way." I was so happy at thirteen to have a word for what I knew myself to be. The word was mysterious and curious, as if from a new language that used some other alphabet. It left nothing familiar to cling to when touching its curves and crevices. Now a word existed, though, and my grandmother was not flinching in using it. In fact, she'd smiled at the good heart and dashing good looks of the bulldagger who'd liked her.

Once I had the knowledge of a word and a sense of its importance to me, I didn't feel the need to explain, confess, or define my identity as a lesbian. The process of reclaiming my ethnic identity in this country was already all-consuming. Of course, in different situations later on—some political, some not—I did make declarations. But not usually because I had to. Mostly they were declarations made to test the waters. A preparation for the rest of the world which, unlike my grandmother, might not have a grounding in what true love is about.

My first lover, the woman who'd been in my bed once a week through most of our high school years, married when we were twenty. After my writing started being published, I told her with my poems that I was a lesbian. She was not afraid to ask if what she'd read was about her and my love for her. So there, amidst her growing children and bowling trophies, I said yes, the poems were about my love for her. She did not pull back. And when I go home to visit my family I visit her. We sit across the kitchen table from each other, describing our lives and making jokes in the same way that we have for over twenty-five years.

During the 1970s I focused less on having a career than on how to eat and be creative simultaneously. Graduate school and a string of nontraditional jobs (stage manager, mid-town messenger, etc.) kept me so busy I had no time to think about my identity and its many layers. It was several years before I made the connection between my desire, my social isolation, and the difficulty I had with my writing. I thought of myself as a lesbian-between-girlfriends. Except the *between* had lasted five years.

After some anxiety and frustration I deliberately set about meeting women. Actually, I already knew many women. Including my closest friend back then, another Black woman who also worked in theatre. I tried opening up to her and explained my frustration at going to the parties we attended. I'd dance with men and keep up a good stream of patter, but inside my mind was racing, speculating on who might be someone I'd really be interested in. All the while I was too afraid to approach any women I was attracted to, certain I would be rejected because the women were either straight and horrified, or lesbian and terrified of being exposed. My friend listened with a pleasant, distant smile. Theoretical homosexuality was acceptable, and male homosexuality was even trendy. But my expression of the complexity and sometimes pain of the situation made her uncharacteristically obtuse. She became impatient and unsympathetic. I drifted away from her in pursuit of the women's community, a phrase that was not in my vocabulary yet, but I knew it was something more than just women. I fell into that community by connecting with other women writers, which helped me to focus on my writing as well as on my social life as a lesbian.

Yet none of these experiences demanded that I bare my soul. I remained honest but not explicit. *Expediency, diplomacy, discretion* are the words that come to mind now. At that time I knew no political framework through which to filter my lesbian experience. I was more preoccupied with the Attica riots than with Stonewall. Since the media helps to focus the public's attention within a proscribed spectrum, obscuring the connections between issues, I worried about who would shelter Angela Davis. The concept of sexual politics was remote and theoretical.

I'm not certain exactly when and where a theory converged with my reality. Being a Black woman and a lesbian blended unexpectedly for me like that famous scene in Ingmar Bergman's film *Persona*. The different faces came together as one, and my desire became part of my heritage, my skin, my perspective, my politics, and my future. I was certain that it had been my past that helped make the future possible. The women in my family had acted as if their lives were meaningful. Their lives were art. To be a lesbian among them was to be an artist. Perhaps the convergence came when I saw the faces of my great-grandmother, grandmother, and mother in those of the community of women I finally connected with. There was the same adventurous glint in their eyes, the same determined step, the penchant for breaking into song and for not waiting for anyone to take care of them.

I needed not to pretend to be other than who I was with any of these women in my family. Did I need to declare it? During the holidays when I brought home best friends/lovers, my family welcomed us warmly, clasping us to their magnificent bosoms. Yet there was always an element of silence in our neighborhood and in our home. It was disturbing to me, pressing against me more persistently each year. During visits to Boston, it no longer sufficed that Lydia and Dolores were loving and kind to the "friend" I had with me. Maybe it was just my getting older. Living in New York City at the age of thirty-two in 1980, there was little I kept deliberately hidden from anyone. Although the genteel silence that hovered around me when I entered my mother's or grandmother's apartments was palpable, I was unsure whether it was already there when I arrived or if I carried it home within myself. It cut me off from what I knew was a kind of fulfillment available only from my family. The lifeline from Grace to Lydia to Dolores to Jewelle is a strong one. We are bound by so many things, not the least of which is looking so much alike. I was not willing to be orphaned by silence.

If the idea of church weddings and station wagons holds no appeal for me, the concept of an extended family is certainly important. But my efforts were stunted by my family's inability to talk about the life I was creating for myself, for all of us. The silence felt all the more foolish because I thought I knew how my family would react. I was confident they would respond with their customary aplomb, just as they had when I'd first had my hair cut into an Afro (which they hated), or when I brought home friends who were vegetarians (which they found curious). While we had disagreed about issues, like the fight my mother and I had over Viet Nam when I was nineteen, always when the deal went down we sided with each other. Somewhere deep inside I think I believed that neither my grandmother nor my mother would ever censure my choices. Neither had actually raised me; my great-grandmother had done that. Grace had been a steely barricade against any encroachment on our personal freedoms, and she'd rarely disapproved out loud of any considered decision I'd made.

But it was not enough to have an unabashed admiration for these women. To have pride in how they'd so graciously survived in spite of the odds against them was easy. It was something else to be standing in a Times Square movie theatre faced with the chance to say "it" out loud and risk the loss of their brilliant and benevolent smiles.

My mother had started reading the graffiti written on the wall of the bathroom cubicle. We hooted at each of her dramatic renderings. Then she said (not breaking rhythm, since we all know timing is everything), "Here's one I haven't seen before—DYKES UNITE." There was that profound silence again, as if the frames of my life had ground to a halt in a projector. We were in a freeze-frame, and options played themselves out in my head in rapid succession: Say nothing? Say something? Say what?

I laughed and said, "Yeah, but have you seen the rubber stamp on my desk at home?"

"No," said my mother, with a slight bit of puzzlement. "What's it say?"

"I saw it," my grandmother called out from her stall. "It says Lesbian Money."

"What?"

"LESBIAN MONEY," Lydia repeated loudly over the water running in the row of sinks.

"I just stamp it on my big bills," I said tentatively, and we all screamed with laughter. The other women in the restroom had only been a shadow for me in these moments, but they came into focus as I felt each one press more closely to her sink, trying to pretend that the conversation was not happening.

Since that night there has been little said on the subject. Yet. There have been some awkward moments, usually in social situations where Lydia or Dolores felt uncertain.

A couple of years after our Times Square encounter I visited my grandmother for the weekend with my lover. One of the neighbors in her building dropped by, and when she left, my grandmother spoke to me in low tones while my lover was in another room. She said we should be careful about being so open in front of other people because they weren't necessarily as fair-minded as she. I was flooded, momentarily, with shock and disappointment. But before I could respond, she heard the words and their incongruity with who she was. She grabbed my arm and demanded, "Forget I said that. Nobody pays rent around this apartment but me."

We have not explored "it," but the shift in our relationship is clear. I feel free to be an adult, and my family has the chance to see me as such.

I'm lucky. My family was as relieved as I was to finally know who I am.

DUKE

Drawing by bar patron (1966)

My father had two wives simultaneously when I was growing up, neither one my mother: Henrietta (my favorite) and Tessie. They lived in harmony and actual support of each other at opposite ends of our hometown, Boston. Objectively, that's the most remarkable thing about Duke. But the list of things I know from him, about myself and the world, weaves around me like the shawls that grandmothers are supposed to make. I feel the nappy wool of his self very close to me: the sensibilities of a charming Black bartender, relatively invisible in an economically depressed city in the 1950s and '60s, in a neighborhood trembling on the edge of something called urban renewal, or later called gentrification. We came to think of it simply as urban removal.

Each weekend I visited him at either one of his two households, trying to slip in between the stepsisters and brothers, stepcousins and stepaunts, as if I'd been there all the time and was not a weekend guest. I did chores. I went to bed when I was told. But it was always clear I was there for him. We strode through the South End as a team, so clearly cut from the same cloth it hardly mattered if we spoke at all. And the charm and style for which he was known was transferred to me almost by default. It was like being the stars of a rhythm and blues song. *Duke, Duke, Duke, Duke of Earl.*

He was what they used to call "heavyset, but neat." My stepsisters called him Jackie Gleason because he had the same build, wore exquisitely cut clothes, and was nimble and witty. It was magical to me that my father was the bronze doppelganger for a famous star. Coupling that with his being well-known and well-liked on the block made him a celebrity to me.

The different thoughts that come to mind to create the picture of who he was are colorful and varied. The clothes, of course. Mohair sweaters, Italian knits, sharkskin slacks with knife-sharp creases, perfectly tailored camelhair coat, worn just the way that Black men do. My favorite look was crisp Bermuda shorts, black knee socks, and loafers or deck shoes. The tempting mocha of his knee showing between the socks and shorts as he glided down West Newton Street turned the heads of most women, and many men. Maybe I liked that outfit because it was one I could emulate. Sometimes he'd let me wear his shorts and shirts or sweaters. Oversized clothes were in, and we'd go walking in the neighborhood on errands or for a drive to get his car washed. Duke and Little Duke, as we were called by the patrons in the Venice Tavern, the 411 Lounge, and the Regent.

He took me on my first trip to an airport. He took me to

my first teenage music concert—Jackie Wilson—because he got free tickets for helping the promoter with security. I never could identify the exact nature of his help, though, since he was hardly a muscle man. He even cried if my stepcousins got spankings. When I went to the store to buy his cigarettes I'd repeat the name of his brand, "Herbert Taretons," over and over until it became an unrecognizable mantra. But Freddie, in Braddock's Drugstore, knew me.

I was allowed to stay up until Duke got in from work. Boston's blue laws usually brought him home by half past midnight. His tip change jangled in his pockets as he loosened the waist on his pants, then held them up delicately with the hand that also held a lit cigarette. The other hand usually clutched a mayonnaise jar full of iced water. He moved elegantly across the room to sit at the kitchen table with contentment written across his face. If he'd had too much to drink, he moved even more elegantly. He was a man happy to have family, and having two of them was only one of the indications.

He, like the women in my family, loved to talk. He'd sit at Henrietta's kitchen table for hours telling stories about bar patrons, commenting on the news in the *Record American,* which he read while eating, watching television, and talking. He would tell jokes with no punch lines, and we'd all laugh until we cried. He laughed until he cried. Turning the pages of the paper, he'd read quietly for a while, then look up at the TV and make a trenchant observation about something that'd just appeared on the screen, like, "That guy (Ross Martin/"The Wild Wild West") has the worst collection of fake mustaches I've seen since Mona Lisa." And Henrietta, Allan, Bonita, Katherine, and any neighbor's kid who might be spending the night and I would fly off in gales of laughter again.

I had weekly tasks, like all the kids, but mine were related to my father's room. I'd spend hours there just being with his

things, reading his stacks of magazines—*Gentlemen's Quarterly,*
Negro Digest, Ebony, Yachting (he read the last one regularly,
though to my knowledge he'd never been on a boat in his life).
I read *The Well of Loneliness* and my first James Baldwin books
from the unceremonious pile of novels that grew and shrunk
and grew beside his desk. I separated his cufflinks, straightened
his desk, folded his sweaters, and counted and stacked his tip
change into the neat piles from which he'd pay me.

I'd play his records as I dusted and returned them to their
sleeves. Then I would devise a better categorizing system as I
refiled them in the newest of the many contraptions for record storage he was always bringing home. One Saturday afternoon he asked me who my favorite singers were. I said Billie
Holiday and Arthur Prysock. He beamed and said, "I always
knew you'd have good taste." I was eleven years old, and in the
thirty-odd years since, I've measured all success against the
pleasure that his expression of pride gave me.

At some point we made a deal: He'd teach me bartending,
and I'd teach him Spanish from my high school text. He really
wanted to learn Portuguese; that's what his father's people were.
But I'd examined the multilingual pamphlets that the Christian
Scientists left everywhere in our neighborhood and I was never
able to make sense of them. Our commitment to these lessons
didn't last long, however. His schedule was often erratic, and
mine became more so as I grew into a teenager. We really didn't
mind, though, since the deal had simply been a device to make
sure we spent time together. That never changed: I'd always
wait up until he got home from work, or when I started going
out he'd wait up for me.

He had beautiful hands which I sometimes manicured. I
loved the cool softness of his skin and the way his hands looked
both masculine and feminine. He usually wore one of three
rings—a Masonic ring with one diamond, or a white gold ring

with many small diamond chips, or an onyx ring with a small diamond in its center. He advised me to never wear diamonds to a job in front of white people. He said that no matter what they said they'd be jealous and not want to pay you properly. He also warned me that gold cars blow up. Not an outlandish admonition in light of the fact that three gold Cadillacs had done just that to him. He'd departed from his usually rather conservative beige or blue Cadillac one year to purchase the gold one. Its engine exploded. The dealer quickly replaced it with another. Its engine exploded. The dealer immediately replaced that with another. It caught on fire. My father declined a fourth and switched instead to muted pink with assorted customizations thrown in, along with a free tour of the big Cadillac showroom for me.

I saw my father intentionally do something to upset another person only once. Every Saturday morning Christian proselytizers would ring neighborhood doorbells to preach the gospel or sell copies of *The Watchtower*. Some people welcomed their visits, usually older folks who received little attention from the outside world, or those who'd been anticipating some sort of conversion for years. But at Henrietta's house it was kind of a joke seeing who'd be stuck answering the bell and then have the impossible task of getting rid of them politely. Once I listened (from behind a bedroom door) to my twelve-year-old stepcousin, Allan, trapped for fifteen minutes on the stairwell unable to maneuver them back out the door. One Saturday we ignored the bell, but my father was half-asleep and annoyed as hell. He went to the front door naked as a bird. The only thing between him and the gospel was the door's glass window panes. It was some time before they called on us again.

When I think of my father, I hear the sound of excited young voices, "Here comes Uncle Duke!" The words would spread through the gang of kids, and we'd be at the door before he could close the front gate. When an adult got desperate disciplining one of us, she'd just say, "I'm gonna have to tell Duke!" All misbehaving ceased. You could almost sense our actual regret at having ever misbehaved at all. I think none of us wanted to risk losing his respect, or disappointing him, or being sent to bed without listening to him tell stories.

My mother, who visited me at my great-grandmother's house where I lived, was beautiful and talented, even glamourous. But she was not one of those ex-wives who was buddies with her ex-husband. She was always cordial to my father, but their relationship was a prickly area we avoided. She had her own family, too, so the two of them remained in distinctly separate domains that rarely intersected—only for my Holy Communion, my high school graduation, or looking at old family photos. But my mother's mother and my great-grandmother thought like I did: my father was magic.

He seemed to know things that others didn't, or accept new information so easily it felt as if he already knew it to be true. He and Henrietta were, for example, the only adults to like my hair when I got an Afro in 1968. Once, when I was very young, maybe six or seven, he bought us each a pint of strawberries while we were visiting his mother. She looked horrified when she realized we were getting down to the last berry and said, trying not to sound hysterical, "Now, John, you know that girl's allergic!" He looked up at her as if he, too, were seven and said, "But, Mother, we wanted them." In spite of my previous allergic reactions, I never broke out in a rash or got sick that time. It's not a bad thing for a kid to think her parents are magic.

When I was in college he told Henrietta to talk to me about birth control. She was embarrassed; I was mortified. It was a smart thing for him to have done because while living with my great-grandmother provided an extraordinary perspective on life, sex education was not part of it. He was only a bit late.

Only once did he interfere in my social life. Not with the Bynum's boy, snobby son of local West Indian politicians, or Dennis, the gambler, but with George, whom I'd met through friends and who lived in New Jersey. I was seventeen, he'd gotten through his Viet Nam tour, and in my crowd that made him irresistible. One Friday my father stopped to talk to me before he went to work at the bar. He said George would be giving me a call but wouldn't be visiting again. I was stunned, but I knew there had to be a reason. He said George drank too much and didn't really have anything to offer me; that he'd talked with George by telephone in New Jersey and they'd agreed I should finish high school before I have dates with a boy from out of town. And he said I was smarter than George. I hadn't realized that last part until he pointed it out. I thought about it quite a bit and was fascinated that someone else, my father especially, could make a judgment that I was smart, that I might even be smarter than another person.

You usually think your parents will live forever. Your world couldn't exist without them. When Duke got cancer, I figured he was still magic, what's to worry. During the last years of his illness, when I was in college, I visited him regularly after class and on the weekends, as usual. The stepkids always left us some time alone, although they still hung out as long as they could listening to him tell stories. Being bedridden hadn't stopped his mouth. Once when I was with him he said rather abruptly, "You know Allan's a faggot?" There was no special inflection. He might just as easily have said, "You know your cousin is a Democrat?" It was much like when my grandmother had used the word *bulldagger:* words from their world not meant to harm but to describe. Of course I knew. I thought of Duke's friends from the bar—Maurice, Miss Kay—drag queens that he regularly served at the bar and in his home. I wasn't sure what he was saying.

"I wanted somebody else to know besides me."

I like that he kept watching out for our futures, even then. I wish that I'd told him I was a dyke and everything was alright, that Allan wasn't in it alone.

Having two wives at the same time did seem unusual to me when I was a kid, but it never seemed unnatural in my father. As I grew older and examined it from all sides I applied the socioeconomic realities, the polygamous theories of Afrocentric culture, the philandering male archtype. I decided none of these applied to Duke. Essentially he liked women, liked talking to them and spending time with them. Something else we had in common. Actually, he liked people. That's why he surrounded himself with them and talked about them all the time. Maybe that was his magic.

He slipped into a coma while watching the Red Sox on TV—not uncommon in Boston (that would have been a Duke joke). Henrietta and I sat with him until the game was over. I hated to let him go.

A SWIMMING LESSON

Hank, me, and Lydia

At nine years old I didn't realize that my grandmother, Lydia, and I were doing an extraordinary thing by packing a picnic and riding the elevated train from Roxbury to Revere Beach. It seemed part of the natural rhythm of summer to me. I didn't notice until much later how the subway cars slowly emptied most of their Black passengers as the train left Boston's urban center and made its way into the Italian and Irish suburban neighborhoods to the north. It didn't seem odd that all of the Black families sorted themselves out in one section of the beach and never ventured onto the boardwalk to the concession stands or the rides, except in groups.

I do remember Black women perched cautiously on their blankets, tugging desperately at bathing suits rising too high in the rear and complaining about their hair "going back." Not my grandmother, though. She glowed with unembarrassed athleticism as she waded out, just inside the reach of the waves, and moved along the riptide parallel to the shore. Once submerged, she would load me onto her back and begin her tireless, long strokes. With the waves partially covering us, I followed her rhythm, my short, chubby arms taking my cue from the power in her back muscles. We did this over and over until I'd fall off, then she'd catch me and set me upright in the strong New England surf. I was thrilled by the wildness of the sea and my grandmother's fearless relationship to it. I loved that she didn't continually consult her mirror but looked as if she had been born to the shore, a kind of aquatic heiress.

None of the larger social issues had a chance of catching my attention in 1957. All that existed was my grandmother rising from the surf like a Dahomean queen, shaking her head free of the torturous, useless rubber cap, beaming down on me when I, at long last, took the first swim strokes on my own. She towered over me in the sun with a confidence that made simply dwelling in her presence a reward in itself. Under her gaze I felt like part of a long line of royalty. I was certain that everyone around us— Black and white—felt and respected her magnificence.

Although I intuited her power, I didn't know the real significance of our summer together as Black females in a white part of town. Unlike winter when we're protected by the concealment of coats, boots, and hats, the summer is a vulnerable time. I am left exposed, at odds with all the expectations handed down from the mainstream culture and its media: narrow hips, straight hair, flat stomach, small feet. But Lydia never seemed to notice. Her long, chorus-girl legs ended in size-nine shoes. She seemed unafraid to make herself even bigger, stretching the broad back of a woman with a purpose: teaching her granddaughter how to swim against the tide of prevailing opinion and propriety. It may have looked like a superfluous skill to those watching our lessons. After all, it was obvious I wouldn't be doing the backstroke on the Riviera or in the pool of a penthouse spa. Certainly nothing in the popular media had made the great outdoors seem a hospitable place for Blacks or women. It was a place in which, at best, we were meant to feel uncomfortable, and at worst—hunted. But the potential prospects for actually utilizing the skill were irrelevant to me; it was simply the skill itself that mattered. When I finally got it right I felt I held an invaluable life secret.

It wasn't until college that the specifics of slavery and the Middle Passage were made available to me. The magnitude of that "peculiar institution" was almost beyond my comprehension. It wasn't like anything else I'd learned in school about Black people in this country. It was impossibly contradictory trying to make my own connection to the descendants of slaves—myself, others I knew—and at the same time see slaves not exactly as Americans I might know but as Africans set adrift from their own, very different land. My initial reaction was, *Why didn't the slaves simply jump from the ships while still close to shore and swim home?* The child in me who'd been taught how to survive in water was crushed to learn my ancestors had not necessarily shared this skill. Years later, when I visited West Africa and found out about the poisonous, spiny fish inhabiting much of the inhospitable coastline, rocky and turbulent, I understood why swimming was not a local sport there as it is in New England. I often remember that innocent inquiry, and now every time I visit a beach I think of those ancestors and of Lydia.

The sea has been a fearful place for us. It swallowed us whole when there was no other escape from the holds of slave ships, and did so again more recently with the flimsy refugee

flotillas from Haiti. To me, for whom the dark recesses of a tenement hallway were the most unknowable thing encountered
in my first nine years, the ocean was a mystery of terrifying
proportions. In teaching me to swim Lydia took away that fear.
I understood something outside myself—the sea—and conse-
quently something about myself as well. I was no longer simply a fat little girl. My body became a sea vessel—sturdy, enduring, graceful.

Before she died in the summer of 1988 I discovered that
she herself didn't really swim that well. All that time I was
splashing desperately, trying to learn the right rhythm—*face
down, eyes closed, air out, face up, eyes open, air in, reach*—
Lydia would be brushing the sandy bottom under the water to
keep us both afloat. As she told me this it didn't seem such a
big deal to her, but I was shocked. I reached back in my memory trying to put this new information together with the Olym-
pic vision of her I'd always kept inside my head. At first I felt
disappointed, tricked. Like I used to feel when I learned that
my favorite movie stars were only five feet tall. But I later realized that it was an incredible act of bravery and intelligence for
her to pass on to me a skill she herself had not quite
mastered—a skill she knew would always bring me a sense of
pride in accomplishment.

And it's not just the swimming, or the ability to stand on
any beach anywhere and be proud of my large body, my African hair. It's being unafraid of the strong muscles in my own
back, accepting control over my own life. Now when the
weather turns cold and I don the layers of wool and down that
protect me from the eastern winter, from those who think a
Black woman can't do her job, from those who think I'm simply sexual prey, I remember the power of my grandmother's
broad back and I imagine I'm wearing my swimsuit.

Face up, eyes open, air in, reach.

IN THE TELLING

Irene Walker and Atia, her niece (1986)

Late one summer night in 1961, while sitting on the front steps of her pregentrified South End apartment house, my Aunt Henrietta and I heard her sister Irene, in the street, shouting angrily. Aunt H. shooed me into the building before she rushed up the block to investigate. It turned out that Aunt Irene, on her way home from a night on the town, had challenged two white cops who were roughly handling a young Black man. They responded by calling Aunt Irene, who is a six-foot-tall dark and massively beautiful woman, a "black bitch," provoking her murderous rage.

This volatile confrontation (including drawn police guns)

has become, over the years, one of the most hilarious anec-
dotes told around the kitchen table. I can't really do it justice
on paper (Aunt Irene towering and glowering; the cops loud
and wrong) because it is her way of telling it that makes it
comic.

So it has been with Black women and humor since the beginning of our history in this country. Comic artistry has always
been attributed to Black men—from Langston Hughes to Willie Best to Richard Pryor to Eddie Murphy—sometimes in such
extreme proportions that Black men were seen as only buf-
foons. Black women, too, have harbored the comic heart of our
culture. The syrupy way Pearl Bailey said "darlin' " and flicked
her wrist, the button-eyed stare Moms Mabley inflicted on a
camera, were the products of a tradition of ironic reflection and
caustic wit that is the distinct signature of Black women's
humor.

Several years ago I was quoted in *Conditions** magazine
as saying, "I think our humor is one asset we (Black women)
have that white feminists don't." Since I made that rash gener-
alization I've been accosted everywhere I go. Non-Blacks run
up to me at meetings, rallies, and readings to tell me feminist
jokes or thrust copies of Alison Bechdel's cartoons under my
nose. What I was trying to say, perhaps too simplistically, is that
Black people, oppressed in this country to the point of geno-
cide, have developed humor as a mainstay of our psychological survival. It is an immutable part of our being, yet a defini-
tion of its form remains elusive.

What's so funny about a Black woman being threatened?
History and newspaper headlines will tell you—nothing! The
assumption has been that Black men experience the most violent confrontations with racist authority in this society. The ex-

---

Conditions: Nine, Vol. III, No. 3 (1983).

amples are numerous, from Emmett Till and the Scottsboro Boys to Michael Stewart and Rodney King. But the Black women who endure the violence of authority remain, for the most part, nameless. The women who were routinely raped by white slave owners were subjected to the violence of authority. As were the four little Black girls killed in the bombing of the Birmingham church in 1963 during the Civil Rights Movement.

Too many Black women come to believe that the violence suffered at the hands of the men in their lives is simply intrinsic to the relationship rather than just another form of violence exercised by someone who views himself as authority, no matter how limited the scope of his domain. Eleanor Bumpers, an emotionally disturbed elderly woman killed by New York City police in her Manhattan apartment, is one of the few women whose name is recognizable. Her death caused no riots, but it was no less real.

But when Aunt Irene tells her story of confrontation with the Boston police, we all roll on the floor with laughter. Maybe part of the laughter is the relief that any of us survive to tell the stories.

Jackie Moms Mabley lasted through three decades of performance from the chitlin' circuit to the "Ed Sullivan Show" and movies, and her stage persona barely changed. She remained a dowdy mess with a profane (and toothless) mouth. Wearing oversized shoes, a frumpy dress, and a cap, she looked like someone's rural aunt up for a visit. But the gist of her routines was to outline her personal sexual appetite, her coda being: there was nothing an old man could do for her except show her the way to a young man. The bawdy nature of her material was consistent with the vaudevillelike routines of her contemporaries Red Foxx or Pigmeat Markham. Her absolute conviction that she was desired, in contrast with her appearance, made a statement about ego and survival that few Black women fail to comprehend. In a society that has conspired to denigrate the value of every physical characteristic commonly associated with Black women—skin color, hair texture, body size and shape, mouth size, gestures—any Black woman who can successfully celebrate the "contradictions" of appearance and desire understands the damage that has been done to our egos and the restorative power of humor.

But what is comedy? People have been asking that question through the ages, and Black women continue to feel out what it means to us. Cheryl Clarke said in that same issue of *Conditions,* "The way we say 'Girl' when we're getting ready to share some gossip kind of rolls off the tongue like a Mercedes Benz starting, and then you know the humor is going to be a monster." Again, it is also in the telling.

And that is not to say that Black women writers are incapable of expressing humor in print. Alexis DeVeaux is quite funny in some of her poetry; Alice Walker in her short stories (particularly in *You Can't Keep a Good Woman Down*); and Zora Neale Hurston in just about anything she wrote (especially her autobiography, *Dust Tracks in the Road.*

When I think of Nikki Giovanni's popular rhetorical poetry of the '60s, it's the *way* she read it that struck a comic chord in her audience. On paper her poetry frequently lacked the dimensions she brought to it in front of an audience. But give Giovanni a chance to deepen an inflection, to roll her eyes, and it's classic comic writing.

Today, when Black women comedians take to the stage to be our poet/griots, often it's still the audacity of what they have to say that tickles us. Like Danitra Vance's bold array of characters, which includes a feminist stripper and a reluctant transsexual, or Marsha Warfield's lewd tribute to her vibrator made by Black and Decker that runs on a "diehard" battery. Or maybe it's just that they, like Aunt Irene, dare to speak up at all. And they survive.

For Black lesbians, making use of our ironic perception of life (from the bottom of the bottom of the ladder) means running the risk of being accused of self-hatred or bitchiness. Since so much humor, any humor, relies on the ability to make fun of oneself, that charge will never be easy to sidestep. When a Vance character pulls her hat down over her eyes and tells us in a deep voice how she became a transsexual when she accidentally OD'd on her birth control pills, the Thought Police are lurking in the audience to slap her with an Incorrect citation. "What's a lesbian comic doing," they demand, "mentioning birth control pills? Isn't she feeding the myth," they accuse, "that lesbians want to be men?" While the T.P. make notes, most Black lesbians who remember those silly dial-a-day dispensers are putting that together with the silky pseudomacho figure on stage and laughing uproariously.

When a Black lesbian laughs at herself, either on stage or in private, it's an affirmation of survival, of her ability to make something from the nothing that we've been offered in this society.

It is especially poignant for a comic like Moms Mabley to present herself in such a frumpy, sexless way, then talk about sex relentlessly. She acts in direct contradiction to the stereotyping of Black women as sex objects by camouflaging her own attractive looks. Yet she presented herself as a sexual being, in control of her life, in spite of her appearance. For those of us familiar with Mabley's life and work over the years, accustomed to seeing the handsome face she showed when not on stage and in the company of women she loved, the entendres more than doubled. She mixed the messages so completely, all the information had to be reevaluated.

The humor of survival is a tactic most Black women have

learned at the knee of our mothers, grandmothers, and aunts over the last five hundred years. Fiction writer Julie Black-womon shows her comic side by using irony in one of her short stories. In it, a woman responds to her lover's announced abandonment of their relationship:

> "No," I lied, in my best Joan Crawford voice.
> "I'm not upset." I chewed the nail of my forefinger down to the quick. . . .
> "So you're really giving up women for Jesus, huh?" I said, and looked up quickly trying to surprise a twinkle at the ends of her mouth or some slight indication that she was only fooling.
> "Well, yeah. . . ." She looked down at her fingers, now entwined in her lap, then back up at me. "Yeah," she said again with no additional prompting.
> "Well, I wouldn't put too much stock in such a relationship," I said.

The story, "Marcia Loves Jesus," appeared in the now-defunct Third World lesbian journal, *Azalea.** It touches on the respite many African-Americans have found in Christianity, the fact that the church has often been utilized as an instrument for freedom: its spirituals as codes for escape from plantations, its membership at the heart of the Civil Rights Movement of the 1960s. Yet Blackwomon effectively uses droll, movie star references and movie dialogue to punctuate the irony of one lover being left for another—Jesus.

Out of a disturbing reality comes a comic reality. My Aunt Irene is notorious for the fanatical protection of her feet, made tender by too much work and too cruel shoes. When my tod-

---

*Azalea, Vol. 3, No. 3 (1980).

dling cousin stumbles close, Aunt Irene simply says, "Gal," in this subterranean whisper that could stop rain from falling. My startled cousin freezes. We all laugh. Aunt Irene knows by now to expect the laughter; she plays to it. Her voice, her knowledge, make her funny. We know she's not angry even though her feet really do hurt.

My cousin looks up puzzled at the wildly conflicting signals she's getting, then laughs too. She's just had her first lesson in Black women's humor. Its roots are found in the West African tradition of storytelling which historically transmitted religion and culture to each succeeding generation. The extended legal prohibition in this country of our right to learn to read or write further reinforced that oral tradition. Confronted with the need to mask or hide their true feelings, a kind of subtextual inflection game was created by Blacks in slavery, which today we have exaggerated and reshaped into something we call *attitude*.

How does an African woman respond to a white mistress for whom she cooks, cleans, sews; whose husband is the source of sexual harrassment; who could, would, and probably will sell her children? When asked to perform some absurdly menial task by her mistress, like Mae West's "Beulah, peel me a grape," the Black woman's "Yes, Ma'am" is bound to be layered with the unsaid. It is this subtext that we're listening for by the time the story is related behind the stairs. We are looking not for slapstick or bombast but for laconicism and cleverness. The humor is as subtle as a Japanese Tea Ceremony and as crude as a four-speed vibrator. It is the "every good-bye ain't gone" approach to devastation. The kind of smooth blow that blues singers like Ma Rainey used to deliver. When she sang "Prove It On Me Blues" her sly delivery acknowledged the fun women could have with each other as well as the danger of such pleasure:

"I went out last night with a crowd of my friends.
Them upstairs womens cause I don't like no men.
Wear my clothes just like a man. Talk to the gals
just like any old man.
Cause they say I do it—ain't nobody caught me—
you sho got to prove it on me."

It's not that white feminists don't have a sense of humor. Pat Bond, Lily Tomlin and Jane Wagner, writer Bertha Harris, cartoonists Andrea Natalie and Lynda Barry always make me laugh. Their comic sense is often like that of Black women—the vision of people who've been victimized but who refuse to be victims. They are good. But, girl, they're just not my Aunt Irene.

FROM THE JOURNALS

Ma/Grace A. Morandus (1950)

October 28, 1982

Today I was unpacking boxes in my new workroom, in my new life with my new lover, still not at ease with the newness or the title—*lover*. I'd never moved my home to be with a woman, and even though I say my motivation is to save money while I take a year off to write, I know that the bigger part is I want to try the grand experiment: to live with someone and try to make a home. Marianne, Sandra, and Davine have gone home after their valiant struggle up four flights of stairs with my stuff. I'm surprised to find myself searching among all the things that have gone so right for something to be wrong. Maybe the room will be too small, or my lover's tastes in food too exotic for my meager talents, or whatever small detail among the hundreds there might be. Under scrutiny, the room remains bright and large. There seem to be no frightening shadows.

I put away cotton tops and shorts that look frivolous, as only summer clothes can in the face of winter. I open the drawer of a small dresser, making room for carefully matched and folded socks. Alone at the bottom of the drawer was a letter sent to me eleven years before by Ma, my great-grandmother, after I'd left home and moved to New York City. She'd raised me from the age of eight until I graduated from college. As a kid I'd never thought living with my great-grandmother was an exceptional situation. After all, I had a mother and stepfather and a father and two stepmothers, all simultaneously.

During my childhood, Ma, named Gracias—called Grace —sporadically revealed details of her own childhood, usually while combing my hair into endless, thick rows of braids. It seemed so mythological that I didn't really believe her until I grew up. She'd been born on an Indian reservation in Iowa. Her parents, Sarah and Archibald Sportsman, were both half-Black, half-Ioway. She'd moved east with her mother after her father died, kicked by a horse he was training. Later came half-sisters Myrtle, whose husband was the first Black police officer I ever met, and Sarah, whom I met when I was about eight, who looked about two hundred years old to me. I was fascinated by the years that seemed to weigh down her house, but not her or her player piano. Edith, a naval officer, was a dashing figure to me when she visited, gleaming with wavy white hair and brass buttons, making endless phone calls. Effie was the sister I never met. But Ma's pictures and stories of her stayed with me through my childhood. Especially Ma's recollection of hearing Effie call out her name one day when she was all alone in the house. When Ma telephoned Effie she was told her sister had just died. I always assumed Effie was hovering somewhere nearby. I knew few others in her family except a wonderful grandniece with the delightful name of Lovey Lovette.

Grace, relocated to Cambridge, was married off at the age of fourteen to John Morandus, who was half-Black and half-Wampanoag. She used to say the union was arranged because she was chronically ill. Her mother, not expecting her to live long, was making sure there would be someone to pay for the burial. She never talked much about her marriage, except when she'd remark with a smile, "Outlived him by thirty." Or thirty-five or forty as the years passed. I never really got much sense of what we would call her "personal life." The smile at her widowhood seemed as much as she had to say about marriage. She'd worked all of her life, in factories and other places like that, leaving her daughter, Lydia, to be raised, in part, by her own mother, Sarah.

I know that men did try to "keep company" with her when we lived together. She must have been in her sixties, but Louis, who drove a shoe truck, would arrive faithfully with his smelly cigars and boxes of shoes and stay as long as she'd allow. And Clarence, somewhat older, genteel and West Indian, would take us to the Fair every summer and sometimes out to dinner. Then there was the white man, John, who I can only vaguely remember. Probably because Grace forbade him coming to visit her during the day, saying she wouldn't have the neighbors seeing a white man coming and going in her house.

None of these relationships felt like romances, although I sensed that Louis, Clarence, and John held out hopes. Grace seemed to enjoy their attentions and conversation for limited periods of time, then she'd end the visit with some sort of disagreement. Her implacable gaze or disdainful retort guaranteed their speedy exit. It always felt like a game to me, something she did unknowingly but irresistibly. I was grateful the behavior was reserved for them and mystified at why they put up with it. It was at great odds with the exuberance that Nana—her daughter Lydia—got from the company she kept. Nana dated a succession of men with wonderful names like Buster and Hank. She stayed out late, played show tunes loudly on her hi-fi, and spent summers in Provincetown.

After Ma retired from the piano factory her life became full of keeping up with me as I managed high school and college. She sent me off to mass every Sunday, although she herself rarely went. She made sure that we got to the annual Horticultural Hall rummage sale early enough to buy me clothes for school, ensured that Lydia, my mother Dolores, and I never forgot each other's birthdays, that holiday visits went smoothly, that we remained a family. And she went to Elks meetings and bingo games every week on schedule.

Toward the end of her life her eyesight was ruined by glaucoma, interrupting the pleasures she cherished: reading everything from historical novels to dime store trash; crocheting endlessly; and watching her favorite television programs—"Name That Tune," "Perry Mason," "Ed Sullivan," "Route 66," and "Star Trek." Faithfully she peered at the screen, listening, and asking me who was doing what to whom. Sometimes I was impatient with the questions. Her vulnerability frightened me. When I left home in 1971 thinking I was finally grown, her health collapsed as if her responsibility for me had been the one strand holding everything in her life together.

The letter in my drawer was written in the halting, careful penmanship created by her failing sight. It was plaintive and cheerful at the same time. I couldn't look at the yellowing paper long without crying. The last time I saw Ma at the hospital she was alert—talking, laughing, and holding my hand like she'd done when I was a child. I almost convinced myself she would get better and go home again. Every week I'd take a late-night Greyhound from the Port Authority to see her. Lydia and I didn't let her know I'd lost the job I'd so proudly left home for. So I told her about the television stars I saw in my Upper West Side neighborhood and talked about my apartment and Jim, the boy I'd been dating the last two years of college. Just before I left the hospital she asked if I were going to marry him.

She could never know how complex a question she'd raised. Jim and I had parted very shortly after my move to New York. But even that was not the answer. She'd never known about the girl whom I'd loved before Jim. Hers was a simple question, but so out of the context of my real life. Or what I imagined my real life would be. She never pushed me toward marriage, even when teachers told her it was impractical to think of sending a "poor colored girl" to college. She was determined I be able to take care of myself, as all the women in the family had done.

Ma worked and survived alone, always daring the men in her life to presume they could make her happier than she'd made herself. Maybe somewhere inside she felt cheated, but she'd convinced me. Once I passed through the adolescent novelty of living out the impassioned lyrics to blues songs, the idea of waiting for "my man" set my teeth on edge. I could hardly bear to wait for a bus, and neither could she.

I can still see Madison Park, where we'd walk together to get to the shopping district under the Washington Street elevated trains. The walk was much better and cheaper than standing at the corner bus stop, shifting from one foot to the other, trying to keep the sun out of our eyes. I would talk about movies and pick dandelions. She'd tell me how they used to "eat those greens, not walk on them," and tantalize me with tales of what snacks we'd have once the shopping was done. We were always moving forward.

I learned to imitate her movement, forthright and determined yet smooth. Her walk, her temperament, her care of me all said she was a woman happy with her life as a woman alone with her child. And that's what I see for myself. For her it was a choice not consciously made. She would never have called it a lifestyle. She simply tried to keep us safe. When she couldn't watch over me anymore, she wanted reassurance that I would have security. So instead of asking if I'd learned well from her example, she wanted to know if I was going to marry Jim. Jim was now only a snapshot in my scrapbook. But I answered yes so she could sleep. She smiled, we held hands.

I put the letter away, back in the drawer. As safe a place as any in the madness of moving. I placed my socks on top of it and left my new room, closing the door on the disarray. I went down the hall to my lover's room where she was taking a nap. I slipped in beside her under the comforter, and she reached out for me in her sleep. It's the fulfillment of a dream, but whose? Not one Grace ever articulated; not one Lydia expressed. I seem to want someone who'll watch over me as Ma did, but how can I tell what that looks like as an adult? As a lesbian? It's like trying to pick a mate who looks like your favorite TV star. You can get the generalities close, but what's behind the make-up? I'm not sweating it. I'm unpacked. I can only trust I learned Ma's lessons well.

September 1988

I'm a little stunned each time I come upon that letter, as if I forget it exists unless I'm moving. I don't remember putting it in the vanity I brought home from Nana's house when she died this summer. The time I found it when I moved to the Bronx I cried like Ma had just died. Now I don't know what to feel. If I let the tears in, I'm done for. That "home" didn't last long (nine months), and the one after that only a minute longer. I really thought we would make it. We felt like two peas in a pod, as they say. Except maybe we were really two completely different varieties. Or maybe we were both too much the same: afraid of being dependent on each other and wanting, at the same time, someone to take care of us. I feel fooled by appearances, not that it was her fault. My eyesight just wasn't good enough to see the signs. Our friends kept calling us a "royal meeting of the minds." That always sounded so majestic, enduring, like I'd finally found the TV star I wanted. A couple so grand the tabloids would talk. Except what was behind the scene? A lot of predigested images of what it should be like and not enough courage to make it what it could be.

I left, and I feel abandoned. Funny how having so many things in common now seems like the kiss of death, or more precisely, a trap. You think you know what the feelings look like. But when she expresses them they seem reversed—love looks like disinterest, fear looks like contempt. A not-funhouse mirror. Being Black, being ex-Catholics, being writers meant little in the face of my being more afraid of losing than of making myself heard.

That first time I moved, up to the Bronx, I could almost hear the drop of rose petals. The next time I felt I was going into battle, but prepared. I think I took too much of Ma with me. I couldn't be vulnerable and strong at the same time. I kept hearing Ma shouting at sweet, crusty Louis as the stench of his cigar floated behind him, "To hingham with you!" She could shout in the quietest voice I'd ever heard. I still wonder what she felt behind that inviolable face. Why did she let him in, then chase him away?

I shout in a quiet voice, too, rather than saying what I need right out, and I blame and I hide. As I'm writing this I hate my lover for letting me do it; just as I'm sure she hates me for letting her get away with being stubborn, unfaithful, and mean. I'm crying over this letter again—for Louis and his losing out, and for me, and for Ma. Even for *her,* still living in that fabulous apartment. Without me.

Now that Ma and Nana are dead and I'm in this strange flat alone I feel like Ma died all over again. I used to think of Ma and Nana as the two pillars at the entrance to the world. Ma was the bigger one, and Nana was the ornate one. But neither one of them managed to get the relationship thing down. And what's frightening is that I can't really tell if they ever really wanted to or not. My mother, Dolores, is easy. She wants to be with a man who'll take care of her, just be there and enjoy life as she likes to. Eating out, hanging out with friends, taking trips. When I was a kid and she swept into our house for visits with her handsome husband, Peachy, I used to think she was so glamourous. But her ambitions are kind of simple and sweetly old-fashioned, really. Grace and Lydia were more complex. Who knows what either of them actually wanted.

I used to believe that I knew them and that the knowing was a triumph, it made me special. But more and more it feels like the important thing was how trying to know them helps me come to know myself. How it shows me a way to communicate who I am to the people I care about, and to the women I love.

I alternate between desperately taking care of the one I love and trying to punish her for not loving me well enough. And I don't know what *well enough* is. I used to think it was having someone to sit with quietly and go food shopping with, as if the simple pleasures Ma and I shared were both the form and content of happiness. There was a level of contentment that Ma had when it was her and me, or her and Nana, that was expressed in a laconic, low-key way. Yet it was palpable. I always felt it. But that quiet was not merely the lack of talking. Her silence was full. I clearly have not learned how to read the silences: I mistake them for caring, when they can be so many other things.

It's odd that this has actually been a very warm and loving fortieth birthday in spite of this disaster. Serena and Carol made me a wonderful brunch in Cherry Grove, Amber and Esther took me to dinner at the most overpriced restaurant on the island, and Lucy and Diane prepared a fabulous dessert. Marianne and Sandra took me to dinner last night; we drank too much wine and celebrated being middle-aged and being friends for so long. When they brought me home I was so depressed about being alone I did the only thing I could think of that Nana might have done. I cut my hair off. It looks quite rakish. Stubby little dreadlocks poking about on my head, pointing to the sky. I was hanging out in the park half the afternoon before Sandra finally noticed that my hair was short.

The look of shock on her face and the burst of laughter made the cut worth it. It reminded me of the time Nana had had a big date and tried to give herself a red tint. Her hair came out so off-colored she was frantic trying to figure out what to do. She finally just went out with the brassy halo and dared anyone to say a word. At least that's what I assumed she was feeling. Like I assumed she enjoyed not having a steady partner and assumed Ma enjoyed being alone.

I used to call Ma every day from my job when I moved away. It was wonderful to try to have conversations just like we did when I was at home. I'd tell her about the studio and New York life. She was always so pleased and encouraging. I tried to write too, making my handwriting big so she could read it. Sometimes Nana would read my letters to her. It was hard for Ma to get down more than a few words. But I'm really happy she wrote this letter. It's something to hold on to when everything else feels so shaky.

In it she says she misses me.

WINK OF AN EYE

My cousin, Allan (1969)

Saturdays were Father's Day for me during my teen years. Living separately, with only assigned weekends in which to play father/daughter, Duke and I made the shape of our relationship through tasks and conversation. I loved the sound of clinking change, cascades of silver—quarters, nickels, and dimes—my father's tips from the Regent, the corner bar where he worked as bartender. I lined them up neatly on his glass-topped desk where he'd count them out and then grandly sweep a share off into my hand. He made a jolly ritual of this payment for my dusting his record collection. We discussed jazz and blues singers and his eclectic selection of books and magazines.

These talks were as much a part of my education as any of the courses I took at school. Just as importantly, they taught me who my father was—a man of immense curiosity and charm, erudition and wit.

His sensuality was apparent in the easy way he wore his elegance, and the soft roll of his eyes; in the subtlety of his social observations and the belly laugh timbre of his jokes. But he could be with women and not have to prove he was a "man." He had no difficulty looking any of us in the eye. I listen for him when I try to create male characters in my fiction and look for him in all of my friends—male and female.

I'm not certain if it's simply my getting older or that the times are changing. As the years pass, it becomes harder to find Duke in male friends. Each year the Black men I know express more bitterness, less hope. There are many valid reasons, of course. Much is made of manhood, and the subtle and blatant ways that Black men are told they will never be good enough are stunning. I see it every day. Although I've worked in administrative jobs for the past fifteen years, it still continues to provoke a visceral pain inside me when I see the disdain directed toward Black men delivering packages. No matter the age or state of dress, they are invisible to white people. This is certainly a question of class as well as race, but the "manness" of Black men seems only recognizable to whites as a threat in this culture.

Working for an advertising company for many years, I developed a friendly familiarity with the regular messengers who were Black. When a white co-worker heard one messenger inviting me to a musical event in which he was performing, she acted as if I'd been conversing with my typewriter table: not shocked, but confused; unable to imagine that this Black messenger was also a man, that he had a life with aspirations and connections to something other than his bicycle and her packages. She also seemed incredulous that I, who'd been lifted up from what she seemed to perceive as the mire of blackness and blessed with a career, might feel connected to this messenger.

Today, more and more, that common bond between me and Black men seems stretched thin. It is balanced less on personal interactions, like the wry wink the messenger returned to give me behind my co-worker's back, and more on vaguely remembered historical events. The '60s was a time when we had official titles—Brother and Sister—as if to negate all the other names slave owners had given us: mammy, uncle, Beulah, Remus. When I talk with heterosexual Black men we speak of The Movement as if it were a shared adolescence that makes us siblings for life. But, like any vision of the past, it's never exactly the same in everyone's memory. And my assessment of the disadvantages of being a woman within the context of the Civil Rights and Black Power Movements is certainly different from that of my brothers. None of them seem to remember Stokely Carmichael's heartily greeted pronouncement that "the only position for women in the Movement is prone." That's not a sentiment any revolutionary can endorse. Feminism has not taken away my pleasure at the hope that period signified for me. It does require me, however, to insist that both political consciousness and action be more comprehensive this time. In the '90s I demand that my brothers look past rhetoric and see me.

With our past in deep shadow, being continually reinterpreted by revolutionaries turned stockbrokers, it is increasingly more difficult to find the shared contemporary experiences or opinions that might help me as a Black woman work with Black men to shape a bright future. There were always several groupings of Black men with whom I was never able to make serious connection. In college there were the strivers, those who I suspected would drop "the community" as soon as the right job came along. I could recognize them by the elaborate efforts they made to keep their dashikis well pressed. Growing up in a tenement, living on welfare with my great-grandmother, I wanted crisp pleats and the right job as much as anyone, yet I thought their attitude reeked of escape rather than social consciousness.

Recently I heard a brother talking about finding a parking garage for his BMW as if that were a political triumph. He'd proudly maneuvered the baroque racism of corporate real estate in New York City, and I felt like the beautiful sweat on the face of Fannie Lou Hamer had been rendered invisible. I knew he and I had taken different paths that were unlikely to meet. And on an East Coast campus I was visiting to do a reading, deliver a lecture, and meet with some of the writing students, the Famous Black Male Writer In Residence didn't bother to show up. One of his female students told me not to take it personally, he never came to the readings that women writers did.

When I heard, in the fall of 1991, that Spike Lee had begun his much publicized course on Black film at Harvard by initially neglecting to include a single film by a Black woman, I wasn't even surprised. In this case, as in the others, I felt as if an artificial construction—economics, academia—had rendered me superfluous to the Black male ego. I knew Duke would have been sorely disappointed in Spike, though. Just as he had been with Black men who feel duty bound on public streets to comment on women's body parts. Or those who call Black women "out of their names," as we used to say. Or those who must trash other ethnic groups to feel like men. There's a level of solipsism pervading Black male culture in the U.S. that Duke would never tolerate and that I still find myself surprised to see.

Some of my heterosexual Black male friends seem to have escaped, or at least curbed, the curse of culture and chromosomes. Clayton, a writer, has known me since I was in college, when he was struggling with his own career. Over the years he's offered the most consistent, uncondescending encouragement for my writing, acting as an editor of my early clumsy efforts, while he wrote for the *New York Times*. He never appeared threatened by my attempts to catch up with him. Another good friend, Morgan, stuck by me in the deep emotional clinches that men aren't generally trained for: when my great-grandmother died, when I was out of work in New York City, when I couldn't figure out what to do next. He was managing a New York acting career, not the most lucrative undertaking for a Black man in this country. But he offered himself and his family as a support system while I thrashed about trying not to drown.

In the mid-1970s I think both Clayton and Morgan, unlike many of my other straight Black friends, saw my coming out as a lesbian as a new aspect of me—perhaps a surprising revelation, but not an invasion by an alien being. They weren't afraid to like me even if our relationship wasn't about sex. These Brothers took their title seriously. Their friendship kept my eyes open for the Black gay brothers I knew had to be out there somewhere.

In the glitter-ball disco world of the '70s, it was difficult to connect with them through the light shows and quadraphonic sound systems. But, as with Clayton and Morgan, it was because of intense personal aspirations—theatre and writing—that I first caught the subtle gay winks of Black men, thrown past unsuspecting heterosexuals, letting me know there was a community. The first time I remember trying to make social contacts as a lesbian it was with Black gay men, actors who worked with me on a variety of productions in Black theatre. I would casually mention the name of a gay club, like The Garage, and we'd glance at each other to check the response. Then, as with the wink from the messenger, we'd confirm our unity.

Until the mid-1980s the public worlds of lesbians and gay men remained relatively separate. Except for the annual pride marches held around the country, we shared few cultural events, clubs, or political activities. But for Black lesbians and gay men the world was not as easily divided. The history of oppression remained in our consciousness, even for some who were too young to really remember The Movement. And since we often were not accepted fully into the white gay world, we frequently socialized with each other. We hung together in the corner at the cast parties and invited each other over for holiday dinners knowing the food would taste just like home.

When I went on the first national gay march on Washington in 1978, I had to be at the bus leaving Greenwich Village at 5:00 A.M. I slept on Rodney's couch, around the corner from the meeting place. We'd come out to each other years before when he was acting in a play I stage-managed. I was fascinated by his Midwestern blackness and the way he paid attention when people talked to him, just like my father. I think he found my Bostonian manners and the rough ways of the theatre a funny combination. We sat up talking most of the night, mainly about our lover relationships and what it was like to be Black and gay in the New York theatre world. It was a world of contradictions, where gay men and lesbians were fanatically closeted and heterosexuals were vying to see who could be the most iconoclastic and arty. When I left Rodney's house before dawn we hugged and kissed good-bye, and I remembered how much I'd missed Black men since I'd stopped sleeping with them.

In reflecting on my friendships with Black men in general and Black gay men specifically, what is always at issue for me, whether conscious or not, is how they view Black women. That, of course, is an excellent indicator of how a man thinks of himself. And my great-grandmother always told me, "Never keep company with a man who doesn't think much of himself." That the male-female sexual tension is largely eliminated between gay men and lesbians allows, it seems to me, an opportunity for both to really see and think about each other, rather than reacting in socially prescribed ways. With straight friends like Morgan and Clayton, and later with gay friends like Rodney, I'm drawn to their ability to actually see *me*, not just see a woman as an object. They perceive my professionalism, intellect, and passion. And in turn they share their own attributes with me, rather than trying to use them to dominate me.

And then there's the unexpected pleasure of being able to view the object created by this culture—*woman*—alongside a man. It has been liberating to see another friend, Dan, let go of the strictures put on maleness and indulge in femaleness. We go through Black magazines and scream at the brown-skin cartoon fashion figures because we know how far both of us are from that fake ideal—me with my size-sixteen figure and graying hair; him with hair everywhere. Dan dresses up in the very things that made me feel inadequate, the things I broke free of: heels, sequins, make-up. In doing so he has helped to create a space where we both can step back and see ourselves as separate from society's constructs of gender. From our perspective, the idealized glossy photographs as well as the other misleading clues about who women and men should be are more easily dismissible.

Because neither of us would give up our blackness, even if it were possible, both of us can paint and primp, don the masks, and laugh at whatever society imagines we both are. We share the wink behind the backs of both the straight and the Black worlds. It's a special bond forged for me only with Black gay men—a bond not broken in history by a slaver's lash, or today by the disapproving sounds of air sucked through teeth.

For many years I've been going to concerts by the Lavender Light Black and People of All Color Gospel Choir. It's a lesbian and gay group that renders the songs of the gospel tradition in the most vibrant and moving ways I've experienced in a long time. What I see when I sit in the audience watching the Black men I know—Charles, Lidell, others—is an abiding respect for our tradition and our survival. They sway in robes I'd recognize anywhere. Yet there is that extra movement, giving just a bit more to the spirit. And that extra beat signifies an insistence that the tradition can be carried on by all of us, not just heterosexuals or the Black closeted choir queens. Charles and Lidell prefer to commune with their people and their God out in the open.

Although the sexual tension may not be there between us, what is allowed to flourish is the sensuality. When I'm with Black men, we revel in the *feel* of being brothers and sisters. We talk that talk and walk that walk together. There is a sensuous texture to Black life: the music, the use of words, the sensory pleasures of food, of dance. We appreciate these things with each other. The commonality of our past and the linking of our future make the bond sensual and passionate, even when it's not sexual.

Several years ago I spent an afternoon riding the train up from Washington, D.C. with poet Essex Hemphill. We both were surprised at the unexpected opportunity to talk for a couple of hours without interruption. When the train pulled out the conversation started with "Girrrrrl . . ." in that drawn-out way we can say, and rolled through the writing of Audre Lorde, Cheryl Clarke, and James Baldwin, the U.S. economy, the treachery of politicians, Luther Vandross, disco, white people in general, and a few specific ones we knew, and broken hearts. We touched these things that have deep meaning for us in an unguarded way, using the familiar gestures and music of our fathers, mothers, and grandmothers. It was a synergy not so different from my intimate conversations with my best friend, Gwen, when we were in high school. And it felt much like those exhilarating moments when my father and I talked about books and music. Essex and I revealed ourselves to each other as writers, as a man and a woman, as brother and sister. We took each other in unreservedly. And we had barely begun before the train pulled into the station and we kissed good-bye.

And now AIDS. The first Black friend I heard had died from HIV-related illness was Robert, an actor. He'd done a lot of television—"Kojak" and other series—and some small parts in films. But on stage he was a tall bundle of American and African energy, large eyes, dark, slightly wavy hair cut close, and mocha skin.

In a play by Adrienne Kennedy (*A Movie Star Has to Star in Black and White*) at the Public Theater (New York), his character was on a hospital gurney during the entire performance. Even in that position he commanded the stage—an able partner to Gloria Foster, herself no small force on the boards. When Clayton called to tell me Bob was dead, it was so early in the epidemic we didn't even know that AIDS was what we'd come to call it. It seemed like an isolated, terrifying disaster. He'd been luminescent, an embodiment of the brilliant talent we each hoped we ourselves possessed.

Since then the grim roll call has grown too long. And again we must draw together as Black people. Until recently, men of color were barred from participating in the testing programs which utilized experimental medications. And although women of color are the fastest growing group in the U.S. contracting the AIDS virus, many of the symptoms that women specifically exhibit are just beginning to be accepted as indicators of AIDS. Thousands have already been left without adequate health care. So that in the horror of disease, just as in the horrors of war and poverty, African-Americans as well as other people of color are unprovided for.

I was a speaker at the Gay Pride rally in Central Park when the New York City section of the AIDS quilt was dedicated, and I walked the carefully laid-out rows where quilt workers had strategically placed the needed boxes of tissues. The beautifully crafted quilt panels went on for what seemed like acres, and my brothers were there—the photos, the Kente cloth, the snap queen accessories embroidered in red, black, and green. And it seemed too cruel to try and squeeze our wondrous survival of the Middle Passage, slavery, Jim Crow, and benign neglect into such small squares of fabric.

I think it is fitting that a womanly art, quilting, has come to embody a memorial instigated largely by gay men. When we try to discern what gay culture is, it is often found in the combination of things that highlight an irony or a difficult truth. When I watch the few popular media depictions of Black lesbians or gay men, I'm disappointed with the flat acceptance of surface elements—campy mannerisms, colorful clothes, attitude—all of which fall quite short of that difficult truth.

When I look at TV's "In Living Color" I may chuckle once or twice, but for the most part the Black gay characters, Blaine and Antoine, completely miss the irony of the new vision being created. The writers seem easily satisfied with their ability to startle viewers by showing Black men who lisp, in funny outfits, rather than drawing a real picture of a Black drag queen, a truly outrageous and complex figure in our society. And never would the writers or the stars admit they might like (if they ever took the chance) these two characters they've created. Their casual contempt shows through. When my friend Dan makes over to look like Patti LaBelle he's acknowledging layers of cultural references that only *begin* with the feathers. He's postulating many relationships to the ideas of maleness, femaleness, and blackness. He is a Black man, and it is *not* an easy laugh.

When I see the AIDS Memorial Quilt I perceive those layers of cultural reference, where they've come from, and how they are expanded when used in this new way. The Quilt is the reviewing of traditional crafts, imbuing them with more poignant meaning. And the relationship between Black lesbians and gay men is also a similar re-viewing of an old relationship. It is sisters and brothers raised on many of the same foods—some nourishing, some not—reconnecting with different spices in the pot.

Such a new dish is not always easy to prepare. Often the bitter aftertaste of our pasts, as well as heterosexual expectations, are too heavy. Even Black men can think they're John Wayne. And a few of us mistakenly imagine we're Miss Scarlet, or even more problematic, Every Man's Mother. In some cases Black gay men and lesbians have chosen to find no common ground and reject exploration of that which history has provided us. U.S. culture encourages that separation. Men huddled together in front of televised football or wrapping themselves in the pursuit of the perfect dance floor are each a different side of the same attempt to exclude women from male life. And lesbians, certainly more than our straight sisters, often find it easier to reject the rejector than to continue to knock on a closed door. More than once I've found myself ready to walk away from Black gay men who cling stubbornly to male arrogance and gleefully condescend to women. Where the connection seems most easily forged is in activities that provide first an opening and then a context for our caring. My reputation as an out lesbian writer and activist puts me in a fortunate position: Black gay men who know my work will assume the connection and the safety in our relationship.

Between me and other writers, such as Essex Hemphill or Assoto Saint or Colin Robinson, the writing provides a path to each other. Our passion for the use of words as a way to save our lives became an important frame of reference for trust and communication. We form a tenuous yet definite community. The great sadness is that with the AIDS epidemic, too often loss is that reference point.

Recently I rode with four Black men from New York to Philadelphia to attend a memorial service. On the trip we joked about how Black people name children, agonized over what we were writing or working on, caught each other up on gossip. It could have been almost any family trip.

The Black minister leading the service at the church felt compelled (in the face of over a hundred gay people swelling his congregation) to emphasize God's forgiveness of our "sins." On the way home, each of us commented on the minister's lapses. But we really were more interested in talking about our lost brother and all the family things that the minister clearly felt we had no right to. We laughed a lot on that drive back, as Black people frequently do when faced with the unfaceable.

I was in college when my father was dying of cancer. Duke never lost his sense of humor or sense of humanity in his hospital bed. He told me with a mischievous twinkle that his nurse, Walter, was the best in the hospital. The two of them kept up a stream of flirtatious patter right to the end. And my father never acted like that made either of them less a man. All that mattered was that he could still make connections with other people and light up a room with his wit.

Twenty years later, riding home from the memorial service with my friends, I could see the same light. Duke may never have been able to envision such a ride or such company for me, but had he been there, he would have laughed the loudest. And I wonder if his wit, like theirs, was one way to withstand life's harshness. Cocooned in the smooth ride of the rental car, the sweet sound of their voices, the ribald laughter, the scent of aftershave lotion, I again heard the sensuous music of Bil-

lie Holiday and John Coltrane I'd learned to love while tend-
ing to my father's records. These Black gay men were comforting and familiar, like the expansive clink of my father's pocket
change.

THE HEAT OF SHADOW

My mother, Dolores (1945)

A gallery of photographs has adorned the walls of my various apartments since I left home. Each of the faces—my mother Dolores, her mother Lydia, her mother Grace, and yet another, Sarah, before her, alongside my father, brother, and stepmother—has in its own turn been a focal point for me. Most often, though, it has been the face of my great-grandmother that fascinated me. Grace, who in her later years seemed reticent to have her soul captured on a piece of shining paper. Her square, Iowa tribal face was often shielded by wire spectacles that concealed her impish humor, but not her unyielding resolve. From my childhood perspective (one I've clung to until most recently), she embodied the security of my youth, the impressive influence of our past, and the endurance of African/Native American women.

Her daughter, Lydia, with whom I was closest in my thirties, represented the possibilities of beauty. In the pictures her face shines with charm, intelligence, and sensuality. I never dress, sing, kiss, teach, or sew without seeing that face, for she was the one who taught me these things. In the years since Lydia died, it is the face of my mother, Dolores, that holds my attention as I feel the slippery departure of my youth. Hers is a face of uncertainty, the unknown. Although it is clear we are all descendents of Sarah, whom I never knew, Dolores and I grow even closer in resemblance each year. Her portrait, among the others, is arch, sophisticated, distant, like many done of glamourous women in the early 1950s. I can see the painted line of her eyebrow, the deliberate softness of her jawline, the romanticized wave of her hair. Her inscription to me, written in 1952, is still faintly visible in the corner, penned in the dramatic script I was accustomed to deciphering when she wrote letters to me in my childhood. What shocks me is that I am now considerably older than my mother was when she gave up my custody and inscribed this photo as a remembrance for me. I don't know why this makes me suddenly afraid except, perhaps, that she was clearly a "woman" here. She represented adulthood, something children can never really attain, I thought. Instead we shed our skins and one day awaken to be another person—the adult. The continuity is indiscernible to me, a continuum that seems tentative, as if we hopscotched through our lives, landing solidly in certain ages and less so in others. Who was I at eleven or at twenty-six, the age my mother is in the picture?

She always seemed as solid as Grace or Lydia in her physical beauty and self-determination. It was only later that I came to realize this was not true. Her life was a mass of contradic-tions, missteps, childish judgments not so different from the ones I made at twenty-six. But I have no child to study my pho-tograph, so who does it speak to?

It is her face that confuses me, worries me, as I step into middle age. My misunderstanding of who my mother was as an adult, and my clear understanding of how society's defini-tion of middle-aged life has changed for women, combine to leave me unsatisfied about my future, even terrified of it. I know some women who will not/cannot allow their lives to be altered by the redefinitions of middle age that have been wrought by the Black Power and Women's Movements. There is always a certain investment in the traditional, even when it is despair-ing and oppressive.

Many women still cling to the comforting stereotypes as if they can transform themselves into Pearl Bailey or Donna Reed—either good-natured complaints or sweet contentment. I have cousins, now only thirty, who, burdened with children and missing boyfriends, take easy refuge in the myth of middle-aged behavior. They, in their youth, know the speech patterns, the actions, the attitude so well that they are haunting in their familiarity. One aspect of traditional African-American culture has provided us with a couple of solid pictures of who we grow up to be. The long-suffering matriarch who gathers her ex-tended family to her bosom and regales them with stories of her exciting yet simple girlhood—the things they miss because they don't exist anymore. She is revered much like my step-mother, Henrietta, who, now in her seventies, has spent her life raising other people's children with a wit and graciousness un-matched by any I've ever met. Her life settled down into mid-dle age, then old age, with a pointed purpose—children. Her role as caretaker almost required her to be middle-aged in or-der to be acceptable. So she may have started becoming middle-aged at age thirty like my cousins.

On the other side of the myth stand Dolores and Lydia, women who had little connection with the idea of middle age. Their lives seemed to me to move as if there were only eternity, and the road map had been given directly into their hands. At family gatherings I did not hear the discussions of menopausal discontentment, the things undone, the anxiety, confinement, or unfulfillment. They seemed to take advancing age as only one other element to be reckoned with in their daily calculations, like rain or a high wind. Neither of their lives was bound up directly with the lives of their children, so the crises attendant upon those links and their dissolution were barely visible. My great-grandmother took the news of my decision to move away from home after college with amazing equanimity. I'm sure she didn't disclose the sadness it brought her because she thought that inappropriate to the natural order. After I moved I called her on the telephone every day; she seemed a woman going on with her life. The few months that remained for her at age eighty-five included a visit to me in Manhattan, as if she wanted to really give me her blessing.

For me in my forties, with no children, no property, no savings, embracing the nontraditional roles of lesbian, African-American writer, and the enigmatic gaze of my mother, I am frightened by the prospect of middle age. If I reject the traditional perception of who I am, who I was supposed to be, with what do I replace it? I have no idea. My mind says there's really no limit. I write, I work as an activist, I'm continually building work and friend relationships. What is there to be afraid of? Most of it seems to be physical: my body doesn't move for me as it used to. While the exercise craze has hit the lesbian community with equal if not larger force than it has the general society, I've managed to evade the compunction to rise at dawn and run through city streets, or submit to the rack masquerading as a Nautilus device. So I may be in worse shape than some, but I refuse to feel guilty about it. My body aches and is stiff. It does not heal. It mocks me with its readiness to become old. And there is a certain amount of comfort in that, too. I no longer can do certain things because my body says so. Will I ever learn to ski? Do I care?

It really isn't the body that's troublesome, though; it's the replacement image. There is none. I'm not washed-up, at the end of my rope, over the hill, on the decline, or any of the other euphemisms, at least not overtly. But what am I? I keep looking at Dolores' picture—the quizzical line of her brow, the direct confrontation of her gaze. There is something there, I think, that might tell me about a new opening. Even if it is one she seems to have missed. She cannot be dismissed because she had a penchant for falling in love with braggarts with unrealistic visions of life. The issues I had, still have, with my mother (about politics and hair care mostly) sometimes overwhelm the deep love I feel for her. As powerful as my issues are, they do not overpower that look. Are there answers for me there? I am as uncertain as the future her look promises. What do I have that will allow me to gaze back at others with such self-possession? Or is it simply a refusal to be exposed?

I take some comfort in my professional status, the publication of my work and my audience's appreciation of it. Such attention is a gift not available to many women even in today's liberation. But to identify myself as only what I do is a mistake that men have made too often throughout history. So what do I make of myself, hoping to embark on new love relationships at forty with a little of the romanticism of the previous twenty years' debacles, but with more of the practicality of a diplomatic negotiator?

It may be nothing more than the fear all feminists must face: how to balance the power I feel controlling my life with a need for support and encouragement. The women in my family seemed to be able to handle only one of these things at a time. My mother let her life be subsumed by her partners'. She chose gregarious, charming men who controlled the shape of their lives while her primary function was to manage the household and to look adored. My grandmother, Lydia, landed at the other extreme. She allowed men to enter her life for proscribed periods of time for her own enjoyment. When they became too intrusive they were banished back to their own apartments, their own lives. She repeated this process through her middle years with a sort of stable of men who never seemed to tire of her attentions and rejections. She was extraordinarily clear about her independence and managed to forsake most expressions of need as if the two could not cohabit within her anymore than she could cohabit with a man for longer than six months.

The ache in my knees and hands makes me certain I don't want to give up that right to supportive companionship anymore than I'd consider becoming someone's appendage. And it is entering the middle years—the aches and the uncertainty—which makes the questions more pointed. I guess I want my answer to be somewhere in my mother's face, but more likely it is in the faces of *both* Dolores and Lydia. The balancing act is what I'm afraid of. My body and my ego feel particularly fragile now while they are in transition from a solid past to an unknown future. Climbing to the high wire to figure out where I'm strong and where I'm needy feels like stretching my resources too far. And I've always been afraid of heights.

Taken all together, the portraits of the women in my family have provided enormous sustenance during the years of my adulthood. Each has meant something specific, has conveyed some particular lesson that I've needed to learn in order to move on to the next phase of my development. The part that I had not reckoned with is the reverse side of the coin: the lineage and triumph they represent is also a burden. They did not express themselves in the same womanly way that I do. They were less likely to articulate who they were and what they saw as the definition of their lives. As heterosexual women coming of age in the 1920s, '30s, and '40s, this was not required of them. It was, in fact, discouraged because they were women and because they were not white. That silence, even as I take courage from their examples, is a curtain between me and what my life after forty can be. And because they survived so magnificently, with such style and humor, they have become legend to me. Their pictures have become icons, enshrined in the naves of my apartments, lending inspiration but also casting a shadow.

I begin to see that my life cannot be fully patterned on theirs if only because it's thirty or forty or fifty years later, socially, politically, economically; if only because I am a lesbian, and they were not. But the shadows that their lives project still hang there, and it is not cool. It is hot with expectation. It makes me sweat as I climb onto the wire and try to see what a Black lesbian looks like when she lives longer than the statistics say she should. The fear of heights is up there with me.

TRANSUBSTANTIATION:

This Is My Body,
This Is My Blood

Me at my First Holy Communion (1957)

I was raised a Black Catholic in a white Catholic town. This was not the most emotionally well-integrated space for a young girl in the 1950s and '60s to occupy. The conflicts were innumerable. I saw the participation by members of the Catholic church in the Civil Rights Movement and at the same time watched the nuns in my St. Francis de Sales' catechism class systematically ignore the few Black students in their charge. I listened to sermons on charity and watched the parish offer fewer and fewer social services as more people of color moved in, and overheard the nuns complain about the "them" who were seeking entrance to the parochial school. Unlike most young Catholic girls I was never inspired to have a crush on my nun.

My great-grandmother insisted on my faithful attendance at mass, but she seemed to adhere to an internal spiritualism grounded elsewhere, maybe in her Ioway roots. She kept a bible and rosary beads nearby, as if living in Boston for more than fifty years caused her to evolve into a Catholic, but she rarely attended mass. My grandmother believed in the Catholic church because of the missionary work on the Indian reservations and because Father Francis and Monsignor Kelly were handsome and debonaire. She found the passion of the church fit well with her own passions.

I, too, was drawn to the passion. Catholicism is grounded in a melodramatic round of torture and desire that must have kept the Marquis de Sade perpetually erect. As a kid I pondered deeply the martyrdom of St. Teresa of Avila, founder of numerous convents, subject to wild moments of mystical ecstasy and profound depression.

And the Christians, thrown to the lions in the Roman circus, captured my imagination. I repeatedly put the question to myself: Would I profess my faith in Jesus or bow to the hegemony of the Emperor? The sensation of facing such a fate vascillated between pride, humility, and an agitation that can only be called arousal. The mythology of the saints and the unknown faithful who chose the lions was seared into my spirit. It was a mythology of ordinary people doing extraordinary things, transcending their natural sense of preservation, clinging to faith.

At the moment in the mass when the priest raised the small round wafer and chalice of wine to the parishioners, the bell rang, and he pronounced the words of Christ—"This is my body, this is my blood"—my heart would pound with the magnificence of such a sea change, such an offering. An edible disk the consistency of styrofoam and a dusty jug wine were miraculously turned into the sacred body and blood of the Son of God, and we were going to eat and drink it! It all appealed to the child's sense of the grotesque, as well as a need for the safety of an authority figure and belief in magic and myth.

As time passed, the miracles recounted by the priest during each mass felt to me much more an indication of the power that lay in the human spirit rather than in the hands of God. I became less certain that one was the creation of the other. In fact, the church looked less like an agent of change or comfort than the bedrock supporting the suppression of independent thought.

There came a moment one Saturday afternoon when I was leaving confession. I'd already figured out that I didn't have to confess the lesbian relationship I'd been having for several years since no one ever mentioned that specifically. But sleeping with a married man was expressly forbidden. I'd just confessed to that sin for about the twentieth time and done the requisite ten Hail Marys and ten Our Fathers before being picked up by my boyfriend (my sinner consort) outside the church when a larger reality dawned on me: I didn't think God really cared. At least not in the way the nuns would have us believe. My teenage confusions seemed transitory and mild in comparison with the transgressions of white Southern sheriffs, the Boston School Committee, and the U.S. soldiers who participated in the My Lai massacre, or people like Jesse Helms, who was a narrow-minded demagogue even then. My heart told me that I did believe in the concept of sin, that it was wrong to do damaging things to others, but my intellect told me the definitions given me by the church were highly subjective.

The interpretation of sin was even more unreliable in light of those doing the interpreting. Although my parish tried, no one could ever make me believe it would be a sin for me to be a maid of honor for my best friend's wedding in her Baptist church. The primitive jealousy with which the church guarded its property—me—even when it wasn't certain it wanted me, made the exultation of the Baptist choir and the expansive socializing of the Episcopal Youth Club irresistible.

I do not now call myself a lapsed or fallen-away Catholic, as the church would have me do, because that sounds too passive. My faith in Catholicism or any western religion did not slip out of my grasp. My faith was stripped away by the years of revelation about the horrors that had been done in the name of those religions. The missionary work, examined more closely, looked like colonialism; the catechism lessons sounded like patriarchy. My faith was rejected vehemently. And even now, with the development of institutions like the gay-identified Metropolitan Community Church, and groups like Dignity that interpret Catholic precepts with lesbians and gays at the center, I find that my spirit does not rest peacefully in any of that religious ground.

The passion of faith stayed with me over time even if Catholicism did not. The church mythology, deeply embedded in my imagination, depicted a passionate commitment to a higher power. That passion was transformed into a belief in human rights and the interconnection of all living things. There's no reason to believe that the weekly stories I saw on TV had less influence on me than the weekly stories (the Gospel) I heard in church. St. Teresa keeping her faith and Robert Culp sticking by Bill Cosby dying in an episode of "I Spy." I'm certain I developed my idea of sin and redemption as much from some of the television shows my great-grandmother and I used to watch—"Route 66," "Perry Mason," "Star Trek"—as I did from the weekly sermons. The passions were the same. It was just the focus that was different.

The first story I published was about a young deaf woman

who inherits a Cape Cod cottage from her grandmother and retreats there in isolation, missing her grandmother and the imaginary friends she had as a child. It ends with her happily crossing over into the "Twilight Zone," so to speak. Her belief in the imaginary friends in a painting brings them to life. Speaking to her in sign language, accepting her as she is, they draw her into the painting with them and create a new family for them all. I was writing a story of faith and the redemptive power of love.

My writing and my activism have become a continuing pursuit of that same faith: looking for the redemptive family, whether it is political or social, that will accept and support me. When I wrote my coming-out story in 1988, I was again responding to the need I felt to celebrate the enduring bond I experienced with my grandmother and mother. I was insistent that the commitment was there, just as it had been between the TV characters, just as it had been with St. Teresa, just as it had been with my great-grandmother, who always stood by me. My coming out confirmed that faith.

Over the past twenty-five years that faith has been sorely tested. Not primarily within my immediate family, but more in the political arena. My sense of myself grows explicitly out of what it is to have a special "American" persona. There is a combination of elements that make me individual: African-American, Ioway, Wampanoag, Bostonian, lesbian, welfare-raised, artist, activist. But the combination is at odds with the monolithic picture many people would like to have of themselves and of others. Blacks don't want lesbians to exist publicly. Gays don't want lesbians to exist publicly. Many white lesbians don't know what to do with Black lesbians either publicly or privately. I'm left to wrestle with who I'm writing for and speaking to. I keep faith with the idea that my life can have meaning for others just as the lives of those who went before have meaning in my life. I must insist that the combination of factors that make me who I am are as natural as the two *H*s and the *O* constituting water. My family taught me that, and it is a belief I hold passionately. I am a product of so many influences: Grace, Lydia, Dolores, Henrietta, Duke, Aunt Irene, Billie Holiday, Lorraine Hansberry, Judy Holliday, Fyodor Dostoevsky, Dorothy Dandridge, James Dean, Audre Lorde, Mr. Spock, James Caine, Metro-Goldwyn-Mayer, and Barbara Streisand. I can only show you where they pop out. I cannot excise them from my cultural inner life, nor do I feel the need to do so.

In fact, my joy is figuring out how they are all interconnected. I feel like I'm trying to take all those pieces, all those stories, ones I've lived and ones I've heard about, and transform them into food for others in my writing.

In the early 1980s I started writing some vampire fiction, which would turn into my novel, *The Gilda Stories*. The book began as simple adventure—a heroic Black woman using her powers to save people, even though she was eternally damned because of her gift of long life. But as the book progressed I began to see that I was reaching for more than an adventure. I was creating a character who, like me, was perpetually seeking that sense of family, something she could commit to. As a writer I liked the challenge of taking a Victorian, predatory myth and recreating it so that it embodied the principles of lesbian feminism that were at the center of my life and politics. Since vampire mythology exists in most cultures, not just Bram Stoker's England, it felt as much mine as anyone else's to tinker with, to reconstruct. And its grand passions mirrored those I'd been raised on in the Catholic church.

Somewhere in the process I understood that my fascination with the vampire myth was connected to several pivotal elements in my life. The death of my great-grandmother in 1971 left me devastated, although it took me years to let that devastation in close enough to recognize it. My loss felt, like that of most people who lose a parent, cataclysmic, as if the world should stand at rest for a moment. In that pain I was seeking a myth that would allow everyone I loved to live forever. Once obtained, the ability to live an earthly life forever was, of course, a curse—I was raised Catholic. The splendid timbre of the priest's voice announcing, *This is my blood,* rang in my ears as I considered the vampiric possibilities. That women have a natural monthly blood cycle made a female vampire irresistible once I started to really consider the idea. The sense of mythology, grand passion, and faith all came together for me in the creation of that character, Gilda, and those she chose as her family.

And under it all was the reality that historically the creation of the vampire mythology was a response to a fear of death. Within that dread was often embedded a fear of life. The preoccupation with the past, yearning for "the way things were," living eternally, were each ways of avoiding the change and loss of the future. In my writing and life I retreated to the pleasures of family life of the past. My family became mythic, transforming for me. This retreat was, I think, at the same time, a rejection of my present and the possibilities it presented.

Gilda eventually had to come to terms with not just her power over life and death, but the places where her power was superfluous, the interaction born of human nature. She needed to learn, as did I, that the connection between people is independent of time and space. Her love of humankind was a highly abstract concept, but in my writing its manifestations had to be specific, grounded in worldly circumstance. Gilda could not kill every time she took blood nor create vampires each time she had an interest in someone. The moral dilemmas she faced were those I'd heard discussed around my kitchen table as a child—family connections, responsibility, our role in society. In the creation of that character, and others, I am able to explore the passion and faith I've come to believe are necessary for living a full life.

As I go into my middle years I find I'm unprepared for the hormonally induced introspection and reevaluations. I was just starting to get comfortable with where I was. After I finished *The Gilda Stories* I was faced with the question confronting many first novelists: what to do with the remaining typewriter ribbons. I was terrified I'd spend the rest of my career writing pieces with titles like "Feminist Performance in the Year 2000 —Art or Fad," or the already used "Lesbian Chic." My dilemma is intensified by the fact that I still feel young, or new to all of this—writing, living, loving. I have only one novel, no academic appointments, no *New York Times* reviews, no movie contract. I don't feel blasé about anything I've ever accomplished. I still feel passionate about the commitment to social change I made thirty years ago. This is my blood.

Making a bridge for myself between that youthful fire and the smoldering embers of the present is frightening, as if embracing the more low-key yet persistent faith of the present could deny the validity of the past. The passion I'd learned to live by was being subsumed under the tiny physical ailments that plague us all eventually. And the realization that there were only so many years left to accomplish everything.

I read a lot of detective fiction and among my favorite characters is world-weary, middle-aged Travis McGee, created by John D. MacDonald. In one book Travis observes that we get about eighty Septembers in a lifetime, if we're lucky. And, put that way, it seemed a crime to waste any one of them. It struck me that by his reckoning, at that time, I had only thirty-seven Septembers left. Crude and sentimental, but I was jolted. My fear of dying leapt out at me, and with it a fear of living I would have never suspected was mine. I think it is my continually renewed commitment to change that keeps that fear of death and of life at bay.

In the early '80s, when the Women Against Pornography activists began campaigning against what they believed to be material harmful to women, some of them used rationales and tactics that were, to my mind, distinctly unfeminist. The efforts reminded me of *The Pilot,* the national Catholic newspaper that regularly published a list of movies too sexy for good Catholics to see. To do so was to commit mortal sin. While I did appreciate the attention to the issue of violence against women engendered by WAP's campaign, their stance was too much like the autocratic denouncements featured in the pages of that newspaper. They had made a decision about what was good for me and what was not. Their activism, and the response of the Feminist Anti-Censorship Taskforce (FACT), inspired me (and quite a few others) to write erotica for the first time. I made myself work at interpreting the experience of physical desire and presenting it without romance or a happy ending. The experience of pure desire, if only on paper, reawakened my world of passion. I began to look at the struggle for liberation from yet another perspective. Because where are those things— passion and faith—located really? In both the heart and the body. I felt driven to keep safe the literature of desire so any of us might have the experience of passion simply by reading a book. And I knew that space for passion must always be kept open in my own life.

The love of humankind was never an abstract concept in the catechism. They said that Jesus actually hung on a cross for days, not berating his torturers, probably thinking good thoughts (if you don't count the *Father, why hast thou forsaken me* lapse toward the end). This is a very specific physical manifestation of faith and passion. My concern that I be able to face the lions was really a need to hold on to faith and passion. Always it comes back to my work—writing about physical desire or political movements. The two will continue to be interlocked for me. The dominant culture—the U.S. government, the church, mass media, capitalism—has had too much to say about my body and my desire as a Black woman and as a lesbian for me to ever be wholly comfortable with it. Agitation for examination of the status quo is air to me. This is my blood.

By the time *The Pilot* list arrived at St. Francis de Sales I had usually seen the forbidden movies already, and the nuns did not look kindly on my questioning exactly what about Elizabeth Taylor or Tennessee Williams might send me to hell. My own family's acceptance of independent thought helped me to locate the sin not in the content of Hollywood classics about desire but rather in the Catholic church's underestimation of my intelligence.

I was fortunate that the family in which I landed was able to give of themselves in a way that showed the value of passionate beliefs and the importance of connections. My Aunt Irene was not too timid to shout at the police, my great-grandmother wouldn't let all the racist remarks about Indians on television pass without comment, and my father cared enough about my cousin, Allan, to ask about him with almost his last breath. When I'm writing I want to know how I can keep those connections going, how I can ask the questions that will inspire the next generation to keep asking questions.

In the writing, when I'm tackling big issues or recreating a larger-than-life mythology, the most effective arena of discussion for me remains highly personal, small, familiar. My fictional characters, even when they're vampires, are always placed within a recognizable context. It is there that the ordinary events of living are made into mythology as I draw upon my own experience to make the ideas come alive. The key is in the sea change: the place where the small incident is transformed into the belief, the daily wine into the blood. In that change I am learning to treasure the things of my past without being limited by them. To use the things of my past without needing to relive them. To make the past a dimension of my life, but not the only perspective from which I view it. In that way my youth is not more important than my middle years; my father was not a god but simply a man able to be special to me; my knowledge is not better or truer than anyone else's, its value comes when it is made useful to others.

For my great-grandmother all things were connected, the past with the present, the present with the future. What she did in her childhood on the reservation in Iowa would relate to my childhood in Boston. My faith may have been momentarily placed in the statue of the Virgin Mary, standing strategically outside the confessional at St. Francis de Sales church, but eventually the faith found its way to my ancestors. It is the same faith, finding its way home. My passion for social change and for the fulfillment of physical desire are the same passion, made manifest in many different ways. On the wall over my desk I keep a changing selection of knickknacks, but always there is a large wooden stake (greatly resembling what Dr. Van Helsing carried into the crypt in pursuit of Dracula), a gift from two friends when I began writing my vampire fiction. Hanging from it is the string of rosary beads given to me by my stepfather, Peachy, for my Confirmation, the ceremony in which young Catholics reconfirm their faith. The rosary had been his for many years, and he was so proud to have me as his stepdaughter, the worn beads might as well have been platinum. I keep these two entwined in my work space to remind me of the power of faith and mythology. And to remind myself of the need to reconfirm my faith and passion with every word I write.

After I left home the church sold the land and buildings of St. Francis de Sales to the city for a new school complex. I was stunned because I thought it was almost impossible to "decommission" a church. I suppose the complexion of the parishioners made its value less certain. I only recently learned that St. Francis de Sales is the patron saint of writers.

SHOWING OUR FACES

A Century of Black Women Photographed

My great-grandmother, Grace, and unidentified friend (c. 1918)

> We are everywhere and white people still do not
>   see us.
> They force us from sidewalks.
> Mistake us for men.
> Expect us to give up our seats to them on the bus.
> Challenge us with their faces.
>   Cheryl Clarke, *Living As A Lesbian**

Hers was a broad, grinning face. The teeth gleamed with
a startling health below her flat nose and nostrils that flared

---

Living As A Lesbian (Ithaca, NY: Firebrand Books, 1986), p.59.

with joy at serving. The bandana, which covered her head, was perennially bright red. Her full lips were parted around those teeth and always appeared just about to issue a jolly welcome. The darkness of her skin was chocolate-rich in contrast to the generally bland-colored and bland-tasting foods for which she was used in advertisements: pancakes, cornbread. *Aunt Jemima* was an image of Black women which was reproduced and perpetuated in advertisements, cartoons, literature, and movies made by film stars from Mae West (*She Done Him Wrong*) to Julie Harris (*Member of the Wedding*).

For whites, the image of Aunt Jemima represented a return to a past when the world could seemingly be made safe by a pair of large black arms and a glistening smile. She was comforting, nonthreatening, and betrayed none of the white man's carnal desire lurking behind his admiration of her. For African-Americans, this image became a symbol of the insidious destruction of the Black race, the means by which Black people could be reduced to being functionaries of white fantasies, deprived of any life experience that was purely personal, purely Black. While the cigar-store Indian seemed remote and even dignified in its stereotypic Native American solemnity, Aunt Jemima could only be a figure of derision: the greasy kitchen ghost not really present until her services were needed, and invisible even then. I saw Hattie McDaniel's eye-rolling deprecation every time I used a package of pancake mix. I laughed at Aunt Jemima's embarrassingly large breasts and mindless smile. My laughter distanced her image from my own.

As a child in the 1950s I could not look inside the image and see the African bones under those high cheeks. It was simply a bandana on her head, not the American adaptation of the West African *gele* head-wrap. The gleam of her teeth was only selfless accommodation, not the contrast of white against African skin, not survival. We were all children then, not so long ago, and didn't see what was behind the caricature. We only felt the pain of what had been done to us in the name of white America. Aunt Jemima was a reflection of what U.S. citizens imagined or wanted us to be, and true to the American penchant for extremes, there was little subtlety. For Black women, the virgin/whore dichotomy in this fantasy panorama reaches its most ridiculous proportions when looking at how African-American women have been pictured in the United States over the past one hundred years.

An examination of the image of African-American women in photography has to consider several aspects of culture that help shape that image. First, because of the racism inherent in the U.S. political and social system, African-Americans frequently act in reaction to white America's behavior toward us. A look at the literature of a most exciting and pivotal period in Black American arts, the Harlem Renaissance (c. 1920-30), reveals that much of the writing done then was an attempt to prove to whites that we, too, were human. Black women were the perfect vehicle for redemption. The work of many writers (like Jessie Fauset and Nella Larsen) featured the fair-skinned or passing heroine who possessed an extraordinary (for that time) education, was from a hard-working, middle-class family, and whose aspirations mirrored (usually fatally) those of her white counterpart. This adventurous but essentially defensive depiction inevitably affected the way that we presented ourselves to others, our own self-image, and who we looked to for role models.

Our visual presentation of ourselves is just as surely tied to the technological advancements of the art of photography as it is to the political and economic activity of this country. Although African-Americans have appeared to be outside the mainstream, we are, in fact, an intrinsic part of the uniquely American flow of events. The portrait studio which sustained the legend of the wild west and documented the elegance of modern living was crucial, for Black Americans, in legitimizing our claims to full citizenship. In 1899, when George Eastman developed the flexible film and roll holder that made amateur photography feasible, he also gave African-Americans a chance to represent ourselves, for ourselves, candidly and lovingly—an opportunity not fully possible before.

Factored into this equation are the frequently contrasting views offered by commercial and noncommercial images. What the pancake box said about who I was remained a major departure from what I saw in my own family albums filled with photos of five generations of women. Reconciling the two views is a life's work for the African-American woman.

Charles H. Caffin said in his 1910 book, *Photography as a Fine Art,* that "[the photographer] must also have sympathy, imagination and a knowledge of the principles upon which painters and photographers alike rely to make their pictures." Sympathy and imagination are elemental concepts in the discussion of any art form, but it's hard to envision a white photographer in the U.S. at the turn of the century with a full complement of either of these crucial ingredients as he sits down to photograph a former slave, a Plains Indian, an African-American woman. We were still an unknown, exotic quantity. Our humanity was still being debated in the parlours and back rooms of the people that had power over our lives. The Black photographer of this period held in his (and often her) hands a simple yet magical key to the rediscovery of African-American history and to the recreation of Black people as full human beings in this society.

As an adolescent I cringed at the unexplainable shame of a bandana-topped Aunt Jemima, but this image was soon counterbalanced by a number of other crucial, yet equally narrow, visions. In the 1960s, Johnson Publications produced some of the most important picture magazines in America. When I journeyed to the beauty parlour to have my hair fried so that it looked deceptively straight and manageable, I consumed, along with *Look, Life,* or *Photoplay,* the magical worlds of *Ebony* and *Jet.* Even *Bronze Thrills* was, in all the tawdriness of its confessional oeuvre, a needed purveyor of female sexuality. The magazines functioned somewhat like the apologist Black novels of the Harlem Renaissance. They presented images that indicated our conformity to American values of beauty, success, and material consumption, and tried to teach us ways that we could achieve acceptability if we had not already done so.

Every month we read about the importance of the lives of famous Black achievers—stars, political leaders, pioneers in politics, the arts and sciences. But the pages delivered wildly contradictory images. We were able to examine how their lives were just like our own as Black people. That commonality was used to inspire a sense of worth in our inherent blackness. Yet that blackness was frequently submitted to comparisons with whiteness and found wanting. On one page we celebrated the image of America's first Black vamp, Dorothy Dandridge (after my grandmother, my first role model), sitting backstage, about to go out on the film set to work her Black magic; on another we were assaulted by the relentlessly degrading advertisements for wigs, skin bleaching creams, and hair straighteners. While the magazines claimed to be devoted to our blackness, they exhorted us to "Relax with Raveen." *Relaxing* became the euphemism for the hair straightening process that would banish our shame as we attempted to erase our distinctive Black traits and emulate the standards of those who hated us. *Ebony* and *Jet* were full of curly or sleek-topped women. The phenomenon was so extraordinary that even the fashion models, usually anonymous, became famous in our communities. Lois Bell, Helene Williams, Naomi Sims were as well known as the products they sold. The magazines confirmed that, yes, we too could excel, be famous, be part of the fantasy world because the famous were not just Bette Davis or Katherine Hepburn but were others just like us. Black performers like Lena Horne, Dorothy Dandridge, and Eartha Kitt were treated like royalty in the glossy pages of Black magazines. Meanwhile, white American magazines paid little attention to this subterranean network of Black people except in the case of The First—a genre unto itself. Jackie Robinson became a legend by being a first; so, too, did many Black women. Dorothy Dandridge was buried under the glamour of being the first Black woman to be nominated for an Academy Award as best actress.

Like journalists' traditional emphasis on exploiting the first of anything (Carol Mosely Braun, the first Black woman senator, or Lea Hopkins, the first Black *Playboy* bunny), magazines used to regularly feature firsts: first Black stewardess for Trans World Airlines; first Black woman hired to work at Washington, D.C.'s botanical garden during World War II; first Black woman to play at Wimbledon or to run in the Pennsylvania State Relay Races.

The image of a Black woman sports figure, of all the pictures, carried a double power for me: it documented the growing acceptance of African-Americans in the white arena, and it indicated Black women's ability to shed the strictures of femininity. Black women track stars of the 1960s were a thrilling reality for me. Their celebrity status was never the result merely of a gift of nature: straight teeth, fair skin, long hair. Track stars were solitary obelisks of achievement. They trained, they shaped their bodies and their futures. They were allowed to sweat, to exhibit heroism, to reveal pain. But their being frozen in the role of Firsts inevitably deprived us of an individualized image within our own communities or within ourselves. We continued to appear as reflections of someone else's needs.

In the 1950s the Carnation and Pet Milk companies sponsored a long series of advertisements extolling the virtues of what I considered the poor people's product—canned evaporated milk. The ads featured Black women and their children and were displayed prominently in supermarkets in Black neighborhoods nationally. But as far as most of America was concerned, Black women were still mothers only to white children. Until the Civil Rights Movement of the 1960s the image of the mammy, or Aunt Jemima, prevailed in commercial media despite all attempts to broaden that perspective. The impact of television and newspaper coverage of another face of the African-American led magazines to begin using Black models and addressing topics involving African-Americans. Advertisers began identifying new consumers for their products. Increased revenue made Black seem, if not beautiful, at least profitable.

The other consistent photographic representations of Black women (from the 1930s through the 1950s) came from government sources such as the Department of Labor, the Department of Public Education, the National Youth Administration, and the Works Progress Administration, all of which documented the presence of African-Americans in U.S. society for archival and journalistic purposes. National Black organizations also created and promoted the use of documentary photographs. Both Black and white newspapers and magazines occasionally printed posed pictures of Black women who moved into white-collar jobs, or the women who became part of the World War II workforce as a result of the shortage of male workers. Just as the image of Rosie the Riveter expanded the idea of who white women were, the image of skilled Black women in the labor force implied a role for Black women in this society larger than that of wet nurse. Such images remained curiosities in mainstream publications, however, and didn't expand the image of who Black women really were in the national consciousness.

But from the first known Black photographer in the United States, Jules Lion (born in France about 1816), African-Americans have been consistently documenting and celebrating our lives. The community photography studio became an intrinsic part of how we communicated with each other. Much of what was communicated was similar to the uplift literature of the Harlem Renaissance: Black women posed stiffly in elegant fashions proving to themselves and to the rest of the world that they too were "civilized." That was not the only message photographs could bear. Among the pictures I have of my family (going back to my great-great-grandmother, Sarah Sportsman Johnson) is a revealing photograph of her daughter, Grace, the great-grandmother who raised me. Grace sits in a car in front of a studio's pastoral backdrop, her face touched by a slight, mischievous smile. Her unknown companion clowns casually for the camera with a cigarette dangling from his lips and his cap turned backward in anticipation of the style of rockin' rappers of the 1980s. The picture is mounted on a practical postcard, which my grandmother, Lydia (Grace's daughter), told me was of a type regularly sent to friends. In the picture Grace shyly reveals a sensual intelligence common in most of her "likenesses." Even in less posed shots she maintains this stalwart amusement. Her mother, Sarah, remained suspicious of the camera. The legends of her people (the Ioway of the Central Plains) warned against the picture-maker's ability to steal our souls. But Grace's pleasure is centered: she may be cautious, but she still offers herself to the camera's eye. These photos reveal a wide range of moods, personalities, physical types, material means, and feelings meant to be shared with family and friends, not just to stand as symbols.

A large number of Black photographers set up studios, or trouped around the neighborhoods lugging great box cameras, dark cloths, and tripods. Many of these were women. In her book, *Viewfinders,* Jean Moutoussamy Ashe discusses the Black women photographers who practiced their craft as early as the turn of the century. The book includes beautiful reproductions of their work, as well as pictures of the photographers. Eslandia Robeson, wife of Paul Robeson, maintained an active career as did Jennie L. Welcome, sister of famed Harlem Renaissance photographer, James Van Der Zee. Ashe, a professional photographer for more than a decade, has her own chilling stories about her survival in a male-dominated field. One experience she had while assembling the material for her book is particularly telling. Ashe interviewed Winifred Hall Allen, a contemporary of the late Mr. Van Der Zee, in her small apartment. There she found three boxes of negatives stored at the top of Allen's closet. They were infested with roaches, and Allen had to be persuaded to let Ashe take some of the negatives away to clean them up. The three boxes represented less than half of her collection. The rest she'd destroyed, feeling that they had no value. Her sense of the prevailing culture's sentiments about their lack of worth was, of course, sadly accurate. But the sympathy and imagination that Charles Caffin identified as crucial to the art of photography certainly can be seen in the work of Winifred Allen and the other Black women Ashe profiles in her book.

The independence of a good number of women during World War II helped to roll back that tenuous quality of our sense of self-worth. The return to "normalcy" of the post-war period did not send all women back to their kitchens. It provided an incubation period so that when the explosion of the Black Arts movement hit the U.S. in the 1960s, Black women were ready for new roles. We had seen those photos of our mothers glowing with self-sufficiency in the 1940s, wearing their crisp slacks and trim suits. We were ready to be the "warrior-queens" that the Black Power Movement demanded. As much as clothing, hair is a major clue to the expanded perception of self that Black women were experiencing in the 1960s. Straightened hair gave way to the old-fashioned, rediscovered corn rows we'd all worn as children. Or, for the really daring, there was the Afro or natural hair cut. Although the majority of Black women were straightening their hair (*Ebony* magazine still receives high advertising revenue from Ultra-Sheen and the Rose Morgan Wig Company), the natural came to symbolize rebellion and pride. The image of Black women in advertising, news photos, even family snapshots, became much more confrontational. We were no longer merely subjects of a labor study, manipulated symbols of a dying culture, or the *first* something. We projected the image we held of ourselves privately, and the camera couldn't avoid it, sympathetic photographer or not. When an actress like Rosalind Cash sent out eight-by-ten glossies for auditions she had no need to limit her presentation. The full-face unwavering stare, the full natural hair, all intimated Cash's independence, intelligence, and seductiveness. She created the image in collaboration with the photographer.

In the 1980s Black women made a comeback in the commercial arena after a hiatus in the '70s. This reemergence was a decidedly mixed blessing. There was less likely to be a bandana now. But most periodicals, including *Essence,* the Black fashion magazine, still favored light-skinned, thin, straight-haired models. Record album covers, which began to reflect the personal fantasies of artists like Tina Turner or Aretha Franklin, are designed primarily within the white standards of beauty. A singer who appears sepia-skinned onstage can look amazingly café au lait on the cover of her latest release. In the '80s and the '90s, though, you might find photos of Black women advertising airlines both in a flight uniform and in a wet T-shirt. They wear the newly resurrected miniskirt or the tight-lipped banker's smile that emulates the "standard" model. The swing to either of these extremes is one we can weather. Establishing a new perspective sometimes requires going out on drastic limbs far enough to get a real view.

Observing the five generations of African-American and Native American faces in my family, the boundless variety of people that we are is inescapable. We wear the bandana, the *gele,* the sleek skirt, and tapered trousers. Our hair is pressed to patent leather or kinky, processed, or dreadlocked. Black women have often been cheated of that broad spectrum by a narrow European-American perspective of beauty, and by a need to veil the Black past and keep us feeling rootless and ancillary. The Women's Movement of the 1970s began to lift that veil, with its emphasis on looking to our foremothers for clues to their, and our, survival. It was in this movement that we rediscovered the work of Zora Neale Hurston and Dorothy West, both of whom created Black female characters of depth and complexity, idiosyncratic characters who'd probably never show up in a magazine photo layout. The establishment of a number of lesbian archives in the U.S. gave concrete expression to the impulse to retrieve the images of women who had gone before. The picture of blues singer Alberta Hunter with her woman lover by her side in Europe, or Gladys Bentley, Harlem's singer and club owner, bedecked in her top hat and tails, found a legitimate home and helped me and other young Black lesbians find our place in history. The reclamation of these voices and images offered not just history but the possibility of a future.

When the extremes of the representation of Black women in the commercial world begin to fold back onto themselves, threatening to drown me in their oppressive weight, I run home to the box of history my grandmother, Lydia, used to keep under her bed. Carefully wrapped in tissue paper, secure in plastic bags, lay the photographs of one hundred years of Black women's life. We used to pore over them together. She would tell me the stories she remembered again and again: how Grace's buckskins were stolen; the night she and my mother Dolores faced down the local toughs; what Sarah's cooking tasted like. Stories told so that I can remember them and pass them on. Those Black faces are an index to the memories of who we really are. She saved them because, unlike Winifred Hall Allen, she was certain they'd be important again.

THE MARCHES

Lesbian, Gay, Bisexual March on Washington (1993)
Photo: Courtesy of Ruth Messinger

I've been on my share of marches. The first I remember was in the late 1960s in Boston. I was just starting college and it was a Civil Rights march called by Black leaders and endorsed by Martin Luther King, Jr. It was phenomenal to suddenly feel powerful in my hometown, not a common experience for African-Americans in Boston at that time. Walking with all the people, singing and chanting, we never forgot that on the evening news we'd see other Black people doing similar things in small Southern towns, and that they'd be risking their lives to participate in this same simple act. Even in Boston we knew there was a risk of being smashed by the water from bone-breaking fire hoses. But it didn't deter us, just as it didn't stop those we watched on the evening news throughout the 1950s and '60s.

My first Lesbian and Gay Pride March in the '70s was not quite as inspiring. I actually watched it from the roof of the apartment building where I lived in Greenwich Village, too shy to go down and join, certain there'd be no other Black people, certain that white lesbians and gays would ignore me, or worse. And even when I got myself to the first Lesbian and Gay March on Washington, I went alone. I stayed up half the night to board a bus leaving Greenwich Village at some predawn hour. A few of the women were very friendly, playing loud music, telling stories; and I heard a tape of the comedian Robin Tyler for the first time.

What I remember most about the ride was that the bus driver was a middle-aged Black man, and I wondered what he thought about those women, about me. He maintained a noncommital expression all the way down and back. But I did glimpse him laughing a couple of times at Robin's jokes. Having my two worlds—Black and lesbian—come together was an enormous leap for me, one I've never regretted.

Two wonderful things happened on that march that confirmed, for me, how important it was to be able to make the type of public statement a march represents. The first incident occurred as I walked through the crowd trying to find a banner I might want to march under. I was moving quickly, scanning the thousands of possibilities, when I practically ran over the parents of one of my students. I taught, then, at The Loft, an arts center in a very upper-middle-class, very white New York suburb. We stood still, stunned. I stared at this husband and wife (whom I'd last seen sitting in the audience of a play I'd directed one of their children in) and blurted out, "What are you doing here?" In my mind I tried to imagine the configurations that might bring them to such an event. (Not an easy task in the old days.) They then pointed proudly up at their placard which read, Parents and Friends of Lesbians and Gays. I was thrilled. It meant my world was not so far away, that I was not out here completely on my own. But then they embraced me and asked what I was doing there. I was quite taken aback. It was one thing for their child to be gay, another for his teacher to be a lesbian! They realized the answer almost as soon as the words were out, and they both laughed as they pulled me back into their arms. I cried as if I'd bumped into my own mother. In that instant I understood the power of coalition: we were irrevocably bound together by a moment in history. A Movement made us related.

Later in the day I reclined on the grass among the sea of faces. We were all smiling. A good many of them were trying to spot people they knew. Once again I felt alone. I knew that few of them could really understand how isolating and threatening it is for a person of color to be so surrounded. But by now I was full of the adrenaline that was shooting through us all and the joy that filled the air.

I relaxed, listening to speeches, scanning the crowd, simply taking everyone in. I saw Black faces scattered in the groupings, but no one I knew. Until I spotted Audre Lorde. She was standing several yards away from me, tall above those seated on the ground. I'd been reading her work since the 1960s but had only seen her from a distance at readings. She was unmistakable, though—the brightly colored African-print cap on her head, her penetrating eyes. I started to wave, as if I really knew her, and continued to watch as she talked to someone sitting below her. Then she looked over and caught my gaze. She winked conspiratorially, as if she knew I needed to make that connection with another Black lesbian. The wink was both flirtatious and sisterly. It opened up a dialogue between us that lasted for more than a decade.

I often thought of the power of Audre's stance among that ocean of people, and her ability to engage me across the crowd. That was Audre. In 1983, when the twentieth anniversary march was held to commemorate the original March on Washington in which Martin Luther King, Jr., gave the "I Have a Dream" speech, the organizers had to be forced to include Audre as one of the speakers. Thanks to pressure from a number of people she was finally granted a place on the platform. Which was only fitting in view of the fact that one of the organizers of the original march, Bayard Rustin, was an openly gay Black man.

When I received the news of Audre's death in November 1992 the image that came to me was her in that crowd, looking tall and mischievous, fierce and flirtatious. It had helped me to define what it meant to be a lesbian. She was a woman who insisted that all her worlds come together, in herself and in public.

In a way that is what a march is about. Whatever the cause, a march says that a group of people, no matter how disparate the composition, can pull together all of its facets long enough to tell the world what it wants and needs.

In 1981 I was part of the New York City antinuclear march, which was actually so crowded we didn't really march at all. I got to know the poet Minnie Bruce Pratt in those hours that the lesbian contingent milled around the midtown Manhattan streets. We'd done a benefit reading for *Conditions* magazine the night before, but it was that afternoon, dancing to someone's boom box and listening to news of the swelling crowds, that the political moment was made. The march became a backdrop to Minnie Bruce and I making an alliance for peace. It felt enormously important for us, as lesbians, to be doing that publicly in the streets of New York City.

At the 1983 commemorative march on Washington I walked with my lover, another Black woman, and I know we both were contemplating what it meant to be two Black lesbians in this particular crowd of people. To be Black, lesbian, and writers necessitated carving out a special place, not simply fitting in, because we knew there were many who did not care to make room for us. The ability to bring our full selves to such an event existed because of all the movements—and the marches—that had gone before: labor, civil rights, antiwar, women's liberation, anti-Apartheid, prochoice. Each one of those movements built on the expertise and political knowledge of those it overlapped with. And each one has helped me define myself as a political being. Without those movements and those marches I would not be able to be who I am, or on a Pride march at all.

I think that many of us would often like to ignore the other marches, ignore the other issues. More and more activists are even too young to remember the historic events that shape their current lives. Some of us don't see the connections between, for example, prochoice, antiwar, and lesbian/gay liberation. That has been a point of contention in each of the movements since the beginning of the Industrial Revolution. Every movement wants to be the center; every march wants to be The March. But the reality is that no one movement knows enough to be the center of change. And each march is simply one part of the grand march toward social equality. Each movement, each activist and thinker, has to acquire enough knowledge to be a successful partner in that change.

Feminism has given us a wealth of important information about how we can look at the world differently. The most significant idea for me has been the value of looking at the connection between all of our struggles. Just as I cannot leave part of myself—Black, female, raised-poor, or lesbian—at home on

any march, no one of us should feel we can leave someone behind in the struggle for liberation. Audre brought her full self
to the public eye; our marches bring together the full range of
what our movement really is. And it is never just the interests
of one segment of the group, even if the mass media would like
us to think so.

After thirty years of marches there is a certain sameness
about them. I've perfected what to wear: wool-blend or thin
cotton socks, depending on the weather; rubber-soled shoes
with ventilation; nothing that rubs the skin; layers; and always
a hat or scarf, mostly so my friends can find me!

Sometimes it seems banal—walking with banners, hoping the media doesn't lie about the numbers, hoping the numbers mean something to those who are afraid of us. I used to
think that we, the marchers, were trying to make bigots change
their minds and make legislators take notice of our power. More
and more that is not my focus.

What I really hope as I'm marching, as I'm greeting the
many people I now know, is that somewhere in the U.S. a lone
person who's lesbian or gay or bisexual flips through all the
channels to watch the news, like I used to do, and sees me or
the thousands like me, and understands that none of us has
to be alone. I'm hoping they will see themselves as part of a
long line of marchers, working to make society a more honest
and fair place for all of us.

The person I'm imagining is not necessarily the one living in a gentrified brownstone, or sitting at the local gay bar,
or just returning from the lesbian cruise. The one I have in mind
doesn't live anywhere near a women's bookstore, isn't really
sure there are gay bars, or lives in fear of losing her children.
It's sometimes easy for me to forget about these people since
I spend so much of my time in New York City and San Francisco, places of privilege for most lesbians and gays. Neverthe-

less, those people are out there, and they are probably the majority of us. I know they need me to be on that march as much as I need to be there and be renewed by all the energy and hope. And the energy is most important because the march is only a brief moment in time. We need that energy after the banners are folded and we've finished soaking our feet and have to head out for the next meeting.

Each year brings more questions for us to examine, more difference to struggle with, less clarity about what the center of our movement should be about. And this is a good thing. The more we are willing to struggle with the issues within our movement, the stronger we are in battling for liberation. The more we acknowledge the many selves that each of us carries to that march, the more we are able to really see and appreciate others. When we catch someone's eye, we'll feel full of fierceness and flirtation. And for just a moment, we can be at the center of change.

DIE SCHWARTZEN

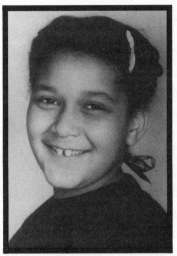

Me (1957)

Across from the tenement where I grew up there was a secondhand shop. This cluttered, musty, intriguing corner was run by a thin old man, "the Jew" as he was called by others on the block. He rarely spoke more than five words at a time, and those in an unfamiliar accent full of open vowels and no periods at the end. In his work clothes he was stoop-shouldered and dusty, like the treasures he had in his little store. His pick-up truck was ancient, as was his small black-and-white dog. They all seemed, to my adolescent eyes, to have emerged from a past which stretched backward into unwritten antiquity and then reappeared in the present on that Boston street corner in

1958 with a puzzled, sooty grimness I did not understand.

My great-grandmother bought many of her important household items from "the Jew." To me, though, he was a mystical being, more than simply a merchant. I was fascinated not just with his age, but with the age of things in the store. Oriental rugs, so intricately patterned—I grew dizzy staring into them. Kerosene heating stoves even older than the plain cylinder that kept our living room almost warm. Bedsteads and detachable mantel pieces for those aspiring to a fireplace. Opening the door to the shop was like stepping into an old world, one I'd read about and assumed belonged to people like "the Jew" and my great-grandmother.

The shopkeeper was also special because he was Jewish. I was fascinated by the idea of strict social/religious codes, and thought I might like to be Jewish someday, just as at the age of eight I had wanted to be Japanese. Instead I was a Black Catholic in Irish-Catholic Boston. I didn't have any idea what being a Jew really meant until much later. I knew there were no other Jews in my neighborhood, and there were few Jews in my school which was inner-city poor and segregated by gender and class. Most Jews I met didn't seem to belong to the same class I did. Those I knew in high school vanished with the other white kids as quickly as possible when the last bell rang. I didn't know where any of them went and didn't question their disappearance. I sometimes thought they all went to those neatly appointed houses in the suburbs that we passed in the summer on the way to the county fair. I had no idea that there were poor white people and poor Jews, too. Still, the Jews were a mysterious people to me at ten years old, as were we, "the Blacks," to everyone else.

When I learned about the Holocaust in my teens it was not in high school, but at the place where I learned so many other things: the movies. I finally understood some of the mystery. I wept and wailed for the injustice and outrage of mass murder just as I had done over Christians being thrown to the lions, and later over the Trail of Tears and Africans drowning themselves rather than endure the Middle Passage. Nonetheless, "the Jew" remained largely an abstraction for me.

A few incidents made the picture clearer. By chance, I glimpsed the wrist of an old woman on the Tremont Street trolley one day. A wrist with numbers etched crudely, yet so precise in their integers. Those numbers signified not just her place in the stream of humanity led to slaughter but also indicated the thousands of numbers that had gone before her. Somehow, perhaps miraculously, perhaps mundanely, the counting had stopped before her number was called. She'd survived as a Jewish woman.

My first year at college, in 1966, I worked as a typist at the *Boston Globe*. One of the writers was away from her desk the day I heard one of the others say, "So where'd the Jew go?" I froze in my seat, a queasy feeling spreading through me; I wanted to become invisible. The phrase was familiar but the sound of it was sharp, like a poke in the back on the train. Someone else answered casually, "To the cafeteria," and the world went on. I kept typing and thought, *What the hell do they say about me when I leave the room?* I was the only Black face on the premises except for the cafeteria workers.

When the reporter returned I wanted to tell her what had been said. I wanted to warn her, to be sure she knew that she was not safe here, any more than I. But I said nothing. I was eighteen, and she was white. I did not dare to mix in their business.

In the more than twenty-five years since that moment it has become harder, not easier, to mix in "their" business. And it has often felt as if it were someone else's business, not mine. In spite of the history that has bound Blacks and Jews together in this society, the division by race has always been equally as strong. And the question of class difference remains a subtle yet persistent one, especially in East Coast urban areas where the Black and Jewish populations (and now the Black and Korean and Puerto Rican populations) have competed for too little space and too few resources.

Living close up makes it everyone's business, yet it remains hard to cross that divide. In 1983 I was in a meeting of a lesbian feminist group that had just welcomed a new member, a Puerto Rican woman unknown to most of us. When we tried to arrange our next meeting, someone pointed out that the suggested date was Good Friday. A white Jewish woman said, "Who cares?" Our new member cringed but said nothing. No one even noticed there was something to be discussed here. Rather than opening us up, the great equalizer of feminism had closed us down.

The reason that feminism appealed to me in the first place was that it offered the opportunity to reexamine each position we've taken in our lives, each of the identities we held, each of the presumptions we cling to. It did not mean that we all had to succumb to a symbiotic ecumenicalism that wiped out every vestige of our cultural or ethnic background. That was too much like the myth of the melting pot. When I watched "the Jew" from my window, cleaning his items, wrapping up the sales, I was not afraid of him. He was unique to me but not an "exotique." I assumed a culture, a family, a life was somewhere at home for him just like mine was for me. I don't know what in this society made it possible to reduce an individual to a name—*the Jew, the Chinaman, die Schwartzen*—and then presume that each of those categories is so distinct it can never have relationship to anything but itself. But that reduction and presumption always creates a distance between me and "them," reducing the possibility of connection.

In recent years, with the rising popularity of the term *diversity*, I see even more clearly how difficult it is for any of us to discuss difference. Although some would have us believe diversity is just another word for accepting into our midst those who are lesser, this country was built, ostensibly, around the principle of pluralism. And pluralism implies the possibility of difference and with it, disagreement. Why have we not made it possible to have that disagreement out loud?

The most satisfying exchange I've engaged in recently was with my friend Lucy, a Jewish woman whose daughter lives in Israel. It was an easy summer day, and we were sitting around the living room trying not to sweat, hopping from topic to topic. I think we started describing how moved we'd been by the arrival of Nelson Mandela in New York City when he was released from the South African prison. I commented on how upset I was that the moderator of the televised town meeting had allowed the focus of so much of the discussion to rest on Mandela's relationship to Israel rather than on the educational and economic issues of Black South Africans. When a woman in the television audience asked Mandela about the future of young people involved in the fight for liberation, the moderator easily led the questions that followed back to what he probably considered the "bigger" news: possible conflict between Black South Africans and Israel.

Lucy countered that the dangers in an alliance between the African National Congress and enemies of Israel were indeed important news. I'm not certain how the discussion developed from there, but soon it was about Israel and South Africa and Palestinians and territory that most non-Jewish women I know assiduously try to avoid. Other friends who were present tried to slow down the pace of the conversation. We continued as if we were feeling our way in the dark, and we were. I understood that we were each speaking from the heart of lifelong struggle, lifelong dreams. We were talking about an embattled country where Lucy's daughter lived. We were talking about a hero whose sentencing I remembered, and remembered despairing that he'd ever be free. We weren't holding back, and still we were listening to our own words before they hit the air.

I felt at a disadvantage as my friend laid out the history of Israel. I had no desire to dispute her facts but I was powerless to make her feel the urgency of my position without seeming to question the legitimacy of Israel's right to exist. I knew that my responses could be as wounding as the time I heard a professor of mine argue that slavery wasn't really such a bad thing.

We continued talking to each other, mostly just taking turns laying out our feelings. The emotions rose, condensing into small tears that settled just under our eyelashes. No voices were raised, yet our responses were honest and strong. The questions were unfathomable: Could we trust a leader who called Arafat his friend? Could we trust a nation that gave arms to white South Africa? Neither of us backed away, neither of us denied the other's experience or blamed the other for her feelings. And the conversation did not resolve itself. We just stopped. But we had listened to each other.

When I thought about it later I realized that a good part of the difficulty of that conversation, and others like it, was the result of (in addition to the specific issues) having our discussion of hard topics defined and focused by men who are usually pursuing a political agenda, men whose primary goal is the accumulation of power, not the resolution of conflict. Issues of power are perpetually being played out as if the Jewish Defense League and the Nation of Islam have squared off at high noon. They each represent extreme patriarchal responses to real oppression, but do not represent me or most women

I know. Yet it is the extreme passion of those groups, as well as the opportunism of the news media, that keeps the public's political focus so narrow. Our interests can never appear to be anything but in conflict, and that kind of conversation is terrifying. Nobody wants to be called anti-Semitic or racist, certainly not by someone you care about. And behind each tentative word lies the possibility of those accusations.

As our consciousness is raised about the pluralism of this society there are more and more opportunities to step over the line into offense. I try not to see that as a problem, but rather as a chance to come up with different ways of thinking about people. It's a challenge to imagine what I might have called the antique dealer instead of "the Jew."

I no longer look at women with the fuzzy romanticism of the early days of the Women's Movement. But I do believe in our ability to make change occur by insisting on our right to examine issues differently from the ways we've been taught. To have disagreements differently, to offer alternative solutions to conflict. When Lucy and I were able to keep talking I thought of that *Boston Globe* reporter and regretted not taking the risk and speaking with her. Or maybe it is only the leap that Lucy and I made with our conversation that makes such regret possible.

The man with the antique store, "the Jew," could probably never have had such a discussion with me or my great-grandmother. The parameters of his survival were much too circumscribed. He was a refugee from a murderous world making his living in a hostile land. We were side by side every day—reason enough to try to have the conversation and reason enough not to. I never imagined I'd find myself writing about him, seeing my world linked to his. I doubt if he ever really saw me, and I never even knew his name.

LYE THROWERS AND LOVELY RENEGADES

The Road from Bitch to Hero for Black Women in Speculative Fictions

Cheryl Clarke, Bonnie Johnson, Evelynn Hammonds and me at taping of
Conditions magazine "Pentalogue" (1983)

When I began work on my novel, *The Gilda Stories* (1991),
I did research on the development of heroic or mythological
characters in fiction. My novel is about Gilda, who escapes from
slavery in 1850, and it traces her life through the next several
centuries. Gilda, you see, becomes a vampire. My idea was to
create an independent Black woman who interprets our lives
through a phenomenal perspective. While the premise falls into
the genre of fantasy fiction, the book itself, like all speculative
fiction, is really about the human condition: loneliness, love,
families, and heroism. In creating a female figure of larger-than-
life proportions, I was looking for the type of character and sit-

uation that the burgeoning aesthetics of feminism had birthed. While speculative fiction has traditionally been dominated by male writers, the Women's Movement has encouraged a wealth of imaginative and expansive writing. Most of it falls into a kind of nurturer/utopian mold while only a small portion of it is more traditionally adventure oriented. But the poetry that has emerged from the Women's Liberation Movement has frequently produced heroic characters, or at least those who seek to adhere to a higher ideal than is generally expected of women.

Where do I find women heroes in a world trapped in the circuitous channels of deconstruction and the smug cynicism of demythologizing? For women, and for Black women especially, this question is posed within the context of a history of oppression and the triumphs and failures that attend it. Within this oppression, the same words used to describe a male hero—aggressive, fearless, unyielding—mean *bitch* when applied to a woman. A man who takes the initiative to control his life, resists the influence of others, and creates his own rules by which to live, is applauded. But because of the restricted nature of the roles assigned to women in U.S. culture, a woman who exhibits the same behavior receives little approval. Young girls are not expected to take to the road, test their mettle, express bravado, or select any of the numerous bold options young boys are directed toward. The glory of women has been said to be in learning the rules of society, upholding them, and teaching them to their children. Deviation from those rules is cause for scandal and ostracization. A woman committed to independent action is a *bitch*, a woman whose frustration has left her devoid of civility and servility.

African-American women have lived with two contradictory perceptions: the role of woman has been both assigned and denied. Black women have been encouraged to imitate idealized middle- and upper-class, white female behavior, but at the same time media presentation, film and print, educational materials, employment opportunities, personal interactions all confirm that they could never truly attain womanhood in this culture. They can never be white or refined. The role of *woman* becomes delimited by racial, sexual, and economic exploitation. It cannot embody a full range of meaning: pure, worthy of honor, delicate, intuitive, intelligent, strong, tough, kind, etc.

African-American literature has contributed to this proscribed sense of who Black women are in several ways. The "passing novels" of the 1920s made a plea for the humanity of Black people by depicting Black women of intellect and sensitivity, but their capacities seemed inextricably tied to how easily they could pass for white—in appearance and demeanor. During the Harlem Renaissance (c.1920-30), the work of writers such as Jessie Fauset and Nella Larsen deliberately drew their female protagonists as fair-skinned, unusually thoughtful, aware of all of the "appropriate" social behavior, and frequently tortured by their need to depart from it. Later literature, fueled by the Black Power Movement of the 1960s, created a curious dichotomy. The movement rescued Black women from the precarious emulation of Eurocentric manners and elevated us to the pedestal of the African princess. The prime role was now to bear children for a Black prince and help give birth to a new African world. The Black female experience was removed from the shadow of white society and reconstructed under the shadow of Black men.

Emergence from either of these shadows is frequently construed as hostility, uppity behavior, disloyalty, and a number of other descriptions that imply that Black women have legitimacy only in relationship to others, either white society or Black male society. It was acceptable for Stokely Carmichael to say in the 1960s that the only position for Black women in the revolution was prone. Any attempt to refute that was and still is viewed as traitorous by many Black social and literary critics as well as political theorists. One need only remember the recent Supreme Court confirmation hearings in the Senate. Professor Anita Hill's testimony about Judge Clarence Thomas' sexual harrassment was drowned out under his cry of "techno-lynching."

There are several writers who have attempted to shift this balance of power, that is, to make the sanctity of a Black woman's life inviolable. These writers have historically been dismissed or denounced by literary critics. Zora Neale Hurston is a graphic example of a Black woman writer whose accomplishments became fully appreciated only in the context of the Women's Movement of the 1970s. Her personal boldness and refusal to frame the lives of African-American women within the parameters of genteelness left her unappreciated for many years after the work she did during the Harlem Renaissance.

Gwendolyn Brooks, widely respected for her poetry, won the Pulitzer Prize in 1950, but was ignored or disparaged by literary critics when her first novel, *Maud Martha,* appeared in 1953, the same year that James Baldwin's *Go Tell It on the Mountain* was published. The book's intensity and social realism was startling to some, a welcome relief to others more in tune with the actual role of women in African-American society. This work reflected what Barbara Christian has described in *Black Feminist Criticism* as the "complex existence of the ordinary, dark-skinned woman, who is neither an upper-class matron committed to an ideal of woman that few could attain . . . nor a downtrodden victim, totally at the mercy of a hostile society. . . ." (p.176)

A number of other writers have found this "complex existence" a fertile ground for their work. For Alexis DeVeaux, a poet and playwright, the title of one of her plays, *No,* and its subtitle, *A Necessary Weapon,* explicates her place in the literary tradition. It is that ability to say no and make one's own path that is the groundwork for heroism for Black women. There are some mythic figures in U.S. literature who break the molds and deliver the heroic characters that Black women hunger to see in literature: Toni Morrison's Pilate in *Song of Solomon*, Alice Walker's Shug Avery in *The Color Purple*, and Audre Lorde in her biomythography *Zami: A New Spelling of My Name*. The world that African-American women characters inhabit has yet to grow large enough to accommodate their complex existence. Neither naturalistic nor fantasy writing has offered enough space where Black women can be *hero* rather than *bitch*. Yet both types of fiction, as well as poetry, offer places where women might throw off the traditional expectations and plant the seed of legends.

The movement that focused a spotlight on the work of Zora Neale Hurston in the 1970s also generated a spurt of fantasy fiction written by women. This work was a departure from a style generally dominated by men, and created a new tradition of women-centered fantasy writing. As I read and re-read some of this fiction, I discovered that Black women characters of heroic dimensions were almost impossible to find. Where are Black women writers like Marion Zimmer Bradley, Alice Sheldon, or Joanna Russ. What is our *Wanderground*? Who is our *Woman on the Edge of Time*? Such an absence seemed impossible. America lives on icons, idealized figures who represent our intellectual and emotional fantasies. We all grew up with them, from Captain Video to Wonder Woman. Rock stars and cartoon characters provide the subconscious guide to society for most Americans, regardless of race or socioeconomic status.

Could it be that Black women were somehow lacking in either epic experience or mythological substance? Is that why none seem to exist in the pantheon of icons of our youth? How else do we explain not having fantasy fiction writers and Black women heroes? And finally, is it really important that they exist? That Black women could be incapable of historic, heroic behavior seemed unlikely. We need only look as far as Sojourner Truth, clearly a larger-than-life figure in our history who might have served as a model for mythic interpretation. But perhaps this history was too immediate, the events of the past century and a half too close in our minds to lend themselves to fantasy fiction yet.

Ancient African civilization certainly yields numerous mythic figures, however, both real and imagined. As Runoko Rashidi points out in an essay on African goddesses in *Black Women in Antiquity* (edited by Ivan Van Sertima), the advent of Islam destroyed evidence of many goddesses of early Africa, but those who did survive are at least the equal of goddesses of other cultures. Many of the European goddesses have even been suspected of being patterned directly after African foremothers, like Neith, worshipped in 4000 B.C. as the self-begotten mother of all, who mated with the wind. Or Hathor, the moon goddess and guardian of the Nile Delta, the giver of joy to all humankind as well as the guardian of the dead. And Isis, the dominant goddess of Egypt, worshipped even during Egypt's Roman domination. Isis' relentless pursuit of the murderers of her husband culminates in the virgin birth of a child who ultimately avenges the husband's death. None of these figures fit stereotypical womanhood. They *are* certainly the stuff of heroic fantasy.

Historical fact is often at least as wild as fiction. The list of African warrior queens makes the comic book *Superfriends* look like Yale preppies on holiday in Ft. Lauderdale. These women were not the romantic, selfless Black queens idealized by the male-focused poets of the Black Arts Movement in the 1960s. They may, indeed, have filled the above description, but they also fit what Marie Linton-Umeh describes in the Van Sertima book as an African woman hero: "One whose outstanding and admirable achievements are diverse, and one who can be defined as having leading roles assigned to her because of her superior gifts of body and mind. And who possesses a number of qualities that most members of the community lack. . .and acknowledge." (p.135)

Some of the warrior queens of Africa have been immortalized by history. The Queen of Ethiopia (960 B.C.), Makeda, was so mythologized that her title became synonymous with regal supremacy: the Queen of Sheba. In addition to her famed love for King Solomon, for whom she endured a legendary journey to learn his wisdom, she was also known as one of the greatest diplomats of her time. Cleopatra (87 B.C.), whose name also entered history as a trademark for beauty, has been painted as a lurid pursuer of Roman bed partners when, in fact, her political and sexual alliances (aside from being fun) were made to serve Egypt. Her suicide was not a result of a broken heart but the act of an Egyptian nationalist who could not bear the loss of control of her country.

Nzingha, of what became Angola, formed alliances with the Dutch to rout the Portuguese slave traders and commanded a body of Dutch soldiers in 1646 and an army of women. Her generals called her "a cunning and prudent virago so much addicted to arms that she hardly uses other exercises and so generously valiant that she never hurt a Portuguese after quarter was given and commanded all her servants and soldiers to do the same." (Van Sertima, p.129) A charismatic leader who regularly addressed her legions personally, she prompted the desertion of thousands of slaves who were enlisted in the Portuguese army. She was named queen at the age of forty-one because she was a shrewd military strategist and charming diplomat. She and her tribe were fierce enough to form a human chain to prevent the docking of Portuguese slavers.

African history has provided the role models for an expansion of our concept of who can be a hero, but few of us have taken a cue. When this store of wealth has been exploited, it has generally been by white male writers who deracinate the history of Dahomean Amazons and turn them into Wonder Woman and Queen Hera. A consistent exception has been poet Audre Lorde, whose work regularly invokes the names and deeds of ancient Black goddesses and leaders. It is clear that the history of African women has many epic figures for those of us interested in the fantasy genre. But why have so few Black women writers been intrigued by either this genre or this history? There are numerous possible reasons.

Until the broad-based Civil Rights Movement, the Middle Passage and enslavement were the most significant metaphorical (and real) events in African-American history. Their far-reaching effects on society have yet to be fully explored by anyone, former slave or former slave owner. But one of the distinct legacies of that most "peculiar institution" was a perversion of the African-American sense of worth in our own culture and a sometimes prosaic proscription of how literature functions. We have been trapped in the metaphor of slavery and its immediate social and economic ramifications, and we are at a loss as to how to extrapolate an independent future.

Over the years the scope of Black women characters has expanded to include the now-familiar roster of *mammy, sex kitten, slut, long-suffering survivor* or *victim, matriarch,* and *bitch.* While the matriarchal or independent characters (Eva Peace, Nanny, Shug Avery, Pilate) have provided what might be termed heroic figures, it is, interestingly enough, the last character, *the bitch,* who comes closest to being mythic.

European-American heroism is predicated on male dominance, usually exemplified by some deed which serves to rescue the female object of his affection as a metaphor for wresting society from the grip of evil. But, for the African-American woman, this kind of romanticism is antithetical to our heroism. We have as frequently had to be the rescuer as the rescued in this society. Romantic heroism implies that women must be deferential and dependent, abdicating our responsibility to perform personally or politically mythic deeds. We must be appendages of men, complementary and symbolic of their heroism.

And, to take it a step further, concurring with Barbara Christian's analysis:

> . . . the stereotypic qualities associated with lesbian women: self-assertiveness, strength, independence, eroticism, a fighting spirit, are the very qualities associated with us [meaning Black women in general], qualities that we have often suffered for and been made to feel guilty about because they are supposedly "manly" rather than "feminine" qualities. . . . (p.200)

This type of Black woman character is, for me, close to mythic. Unlike traditional female figures, even those Black women who are strong survivors, the bitch is the center of her own world. She controls her life and will stop at little to achieve her goals. Such a character is Cleo Judson in Dorothy West's *The Living Is Easy,* originally published in 1948. Cleo, born of modest means, is majestic, disdainful, self-centered. She schemes to outwit everyone, including her husband, and wrings profits from whomever she can. She is self-preservation run amok. Yet in spite of these extremes, or maybe because of them, Cleo is one of the most compelling characters in our literary history. She is self-aware in a fanatical way. Her underlying knowledge of society's lack of room for her independence turns her aspirations to bitter machinations. She is barely able to contain her feelings of exclusion and disenfranchisement:

> *Cleo felt a sharp distaste at the surge and clangor around her that made her pause at every storefront where a man might come charging out of a doorway to brush aside any women or children who stood in the path of commerce. Here in the market was all the maleness of men. This was their world in which they moved without the command of women. . .Curses ran lightly over their lips, wonderful expressive words that Cleo stored in the back of her head.* (p.70)

As I read I was amazed at the cleverness and ruthlessness of each deed, often hoping against hope that Cleo will repent and do something for "the greater good." Instead, she rewrites rent receipts in order to pocket twenty dollars every time her husband pays the landlord, deliberately turns her sisters against her stepmother in a plot to persuade them to come live with her, and perpetually upbraids her daughter and her darker-skinned husband for not living up to her standards. And although she, unlike Scarlet O'Hara (another great *bitch* figure), never does "do the right thing," the character certainly has resonance worthy of her name.

Although her mythic deeds are largely negative, Cleo lives as a quintessential legendary character. Her refusal to stay within her established role as Black woman necessitates her use of deviousness and callous self-interest. She can see no other way to disobey.

The acute need to break the rules of behavior in order to live as a whole person is not confined to African-Americans but is manifest in most African women living within Eurocentric parameters. Barbara Burford, a British Black woman of Caribbean descent, writes of this need repeatedly in her collection of short stories, *The Threshing Floor* (1989). The transition from being an ordinary Black *bitch* to becoming a Black *hero* is not simply a turning of a corner. It is a leap. And the first step toward that precipitous leap is the simple act of disobedience. Just as slaves learned that to live as human they had to be creatively disobedient so, too, have Black women had to reexamine their relationship to accepted behavior. In Burford's stories the leaps are relatively modest breaks with the subtle expectations that routinely oppress women rather than the complex strategies executed by Cleo Judson.

Dorothy, a mature secretary in "Pinstripe Summer," reaches past her narrow-minded, white boss and the fear of technology to embrace the advent of the computer age. At the same time, she makes a new friend of the younger Black woman who comes to teach her about computers. Parallel to this awakening is Dorothy's growing obsession with a mysterious grove that she passes every day on the commuter train to work. Eventually she gains personal strength because of her new confidence at work. It inspires her to leave the train before her stop in order to explore the alien landscape of trees and brush that has beckoned to her. As she climbs through the brambles she repeats what she calls "the dreadful repressive litanies of her upbringing": "Ladies do not wear trousers. Ladies do not ride bicycles. Ladies do not cross their legs." (p.25) Dorothy remembers all the admonitions as she promises herself a pair of slacks. It is a simple act of rebellion for a Black woman accustomed to trying to fit into white society. Burford's perspective, that of being Black in Britain, helps her construct this powerful need to break with tradition in a way not too dissimilar from Cleo Judson's. The difference is in the period of history, Dorothy's connection to the independent women, and the options these elements offer.

Each of Burford's characters is trying to take that first step. In one story a little girl rebels against being told by white teachers that she is fat and clumsy by learning to fly. In the title story a Black woman recovering from the death of her white woman lover learns to make a place for herself in the white village in which they'd lived. Each character must break with demands or expectations and find her own way to individuality. And, in many cases, that break must be harsh or, as with the child who learns to fly, extraordinary. Burford writes in a very naturalistic way but frequently uses fantastic or surrealistic elements to point toward the path of independence. This quality, a natural part of any Afrocentric culture, gives Burford's characters the space to surpass the limitations presented them without resorting to pure trickery.

In any African-based culture, there will always be one figure with the potential for that mythic status, the conjure woman. She has been explored tangentially in African-American literature on occasion. Several stories by Alice Walker (*In Love and Trouble,* 1973) and others use the conjure woman as an otherworldly force whose magical capabilities are both fearful and awe-inspiring. But the conjure woman has not yet become a staple in fantasy fiction. Marie Le Veau, the leading practitioner of voudun in New Orleans and in this country, remains a mythic prototype awaiting the birth of her progeny, for example. As a figure of such majestic disavowal of female roles it is not unexpected that little written material is available from traditional information sources. Additionally, the figures of the conjure woman and Marie Le Veau represent a rebellion not only against their designated roles as women but also as departures from the tradition of Christianity, an uneasy position even today in this society.

And, of course, the previously noted demand (whether explicit or implicit) that art serve politics is a further consequence of that history. The unwieldy figure of the conjure woman and discomforting reality of Marie Le Veau do not make good servants. Ironically, as we serve politics our writing is also reflecting politics. The sexism in our society is also sexism in our creative thinking.

The inability to see ourselves as the center of anything, even our own lives, has in one sense allowed Black women to be the backbone of Black communities, but it has also limited our perspective on the world and that of our literary critics. In an issue of *The Black Scholar* Calvin Hernton described the scurrilous attack mounted against Ntozake Shange by Black critics after the production of her play/choreopoem, *For Colored Girls Who Have Considered Suicide When the Rainbow Is Enuf.* She was called man-hating, a rip-off, and a pawn of white people in the destruction of Black malehood.

What was really infuriating to her critics, however, was not that her poems libeled Black men (they did not) but that men were not central figures in them. Some critics pointed to the poem "Beau Willie Brown" (a dramatic depiction of a Black man driven to madness and infanticide by poverty, lack of education, and his experiences in Viet Nam) as a subversive assault on Black men. In doing so they conveniently ignored the loving portraits Shange drew of other Black men, such as artists Oliver Lake, Willie Colon, Archie Shepp, and Hector Lavoe. They also completely dismiss her profound tribute to Toussaint L'Overture, in which the little girl narrator asserts Toussaint "waz the beginnin uv reality for me. . . ." (p.27)

This poem and others show Shange's intricate weaving of Black history and Black family into her own liberation as a woman. The real scandal to her detractors (and to those of Alice Walker's *The Color Purple* a decade later) was that most of her poems were not really about men at all. Rather they were an exploration of female commonality. While men may have been present, the Black woman's experience was the center at all times. A departure, a heroic stance, not commonly accepted in Black women. And where Black men do exhibit negative behavior in the poems, the response of Black women is never passive or accepting, but rather angry and disappointed.

Hernton locates the source of the disturbance for the many Black dissenters: a Black woman writer's declaration of autonomy and refusal to adhere to the tradition of making Black female feelings and concerns secondary to those of Black men. He acknowledges what Black women writers who are involved in feminist and lesbian publishing have known all along: "The literature of contemporary black women is a dialectical composite of the unknown coming out of the known. It is an upheaval in form, style and landscape. It is the negation of the negative and it proffers a vision of unfettered human possibility." (p.58)

This vision of "unfettered human possibility" is, indeed, what fantasy fiction is all about, and, by virtue of its form as well as its content this is also true of contemporary poetry.

Two pieces of fiction by Black writers Octavia Butler and Michelle Parkerson began to open up this vision for me. These writers eschew the centuries-old idea (as Barbara Christian points out) which dictates that heroism for women consists largely of being physically beautiful and overtly compliant.

In Butler's 1979 novel, *Kindred,* the primary character, Dana (a Black woman), mysteriously and literally vanishes from her modern urban home to reappear on a nineteenth-century plantation in time to save the life of the plantation owner's drowning son. She is drawn repeatedly into the past, involuntarily, to save the life of the white boy who soon becomes a man. Her discovery that his survival is key to the birth of an ancestor of hers gives the rescues their dramatic glue. Dana becomes an inexplicable fixture, reappearing over the years on the plantation and providing the slaves with a magical, legendary character. Throughout the story Dana is distinguished by her refusal to react in any traditionally prescribed way. She consistently responds to physical danger with both acuity and strength. She uses logic and cunning, relying on hard facts as well as her own intuition. She never casts others in the role of her protector.

Of course, part of Dana's strength comes from the knowledge that there is another century to which she can return when the conditions exist that allow her to travel. She is unbowed, to some extent, by the punitive circumstances of slavery because escape awaits her more easily than the others. But her assertiveness and wisdom are part of her personality in both worlds. As if to truly challenge Dana, the author has given her several patriarchal figures to overcome: her husband, a young white writer, who, in spite of his sensitivity, is perpetually naive and has no real idea of what this experience does to his wife, physically and psychologically. There is also the petulant boy who grows into an egocentric and cruel slave owner, and the boy's father who remains confounded by Dana's bewitching appearances and dangerously limited by his ignorance.

On Dana's final summoning to save the boy from a drunken accident, it is clear what sort of dissolute wastrel he has become. Yet her response continues to be humane as long as he remembers her humanity. When he assaults her and attempts to rape her, she kills him with little compunction. It is an act not of cruelty but of survival—cleanly done—leaving her with sadness at the taking of life but no disavowal of her right to protect herself. She resorts to no stereotypical shrinking or shrieking, no abdication of responsibility for her own life. This is a mythic hero, traditional in her direct response to personal and social danger yet "feminine" in her refusal to disengage her emotions from the actions.

Butler is admirable in her ability to avoid the idealized concepts of heroism in her writing. Dana acknowledges her emotional needs but is not paralyzed by them. The author does not create an idyllic interracial marriage or overly sympathetic husband. Dana, the hero, acts out of both the ordinary and the extraordinary.

Another story that exhibits a similiar quality of heroism emerging from ordinary emotional circumstance is a very short one by Michelle Parkerson. Entitled "Odds and Ends, a New Amazon Fable," it appears in her collection of poetry and prose, *Waiting Rooms* (1983). It is set in 2036 while a war is raging, and exists almost as a snapshot of two women warriors, Loz and Sephra, who are lovers. Parkerson extrapolates the future from our violent past: "The race wars of earth escalated to cosmic insurrection. Colored peoples everywhere had taken enough and took up arms." (p.7) The warriors here are women sustaining a pitched battle against invasion and trying to maintain some semblance of personal life.

The world at war is a traditional format for creating heroic figures although the segregation of the sexes has left women almost entirely out of that picture except as nurses. Here Loz is a "reluctant warrior" who lingers in the love of her sister warrior. After returning from a three-day pass such love keeps her "dancing or killing, when all else fails." (p.6) Parkerson uses her skills as a poet to make the colors of love and war vibrate for us throughout the story. She turns the familiar into mythology: the Seventh sector is demarcated by Squeak's Bar-B-Q and Miss Edna's Curla Palace. And the warriors are not Rambo but women whose concern for each other is shown in personalized interdependence as well as military responsibility.

Sephra is the "last in a notorious line of lye throwers and lovely renegades." (p.8) Although the scent of love is still fresh when the vandals break through the lines and overrun her base camp, Sephra loses no time springing into action. Sentiment is not allowed to dominate her final note to Loz: "I am a child of dread, born of veiled face and master number/a sable eyeful of Loz and Armageddon . . . ." (p.10) Her message of love is transmitted while she detonates the grenade which breaks the ranks of the enemy and ends her life. Sephra takes her place as a true descendent of Cleopatra and Nzingha. Here, just as *the bitch* makes her own existence the center of her life, *the hero* makes survival of the whole an extension of herself, the center of her being. Not financial security, not men, not approval, not any of the things that traditionally relegate Black women to the uncomfortable balance on the pedestal or to the rearguard vantage point of the kitchen.

Having learned that such women heroes can exist, we must ask whether it is at all important for us to look for or create them in our fiction. It's not an accident that at moments of political upheaval fantasy or science fiction writing has taken on a greater resonance for the public. George Orwell's *1984* was the fruit of post World War II devastation and the chilling reality of the atom bomb. During the turbulence of the Civil Rights and Anti-War Movements of the 1960s and '70s fantasy fiction again regained popularity (*Stranger in a Strange Land,* Asimov's *Foundation* series) as those hoping to destroy oppressive traditions looked to the future for utopian visions. And the Women's Movement has spawned a healthy body of fantasy fiction work, replacing the images of passive victims and strident agitators with shrewd warriors and hopeful women activists.

A great many of these have been lesbian characters, rich with the "stereotyped" qualities that Christian described: "fighting spirit, strength, eroticism." (p.200) All Black women hunger for that vision of independent heroics. It has more often been supplied by our poets. Poetry has historically been used for epic narrative and has often been utilized by those at the vanguard of liberation movements to educate and inspire. The Women's Movement is no exception. Poetry's nonlinear quality and lyric elements provide a ready base for the leap that women need to make. To be heroic or mythic within that context for women in general, and Black women specifically, means the ability to be part of the survival of a community in the manner we choose. At the same time to keep one eye turned toward our own survival as Black women. This requires a clarity about responsibility not only to the whole but to the visionary possibilities of the individual. Writers such as Audre Lorde, Alexis DeVeaux, Colleen J. McElroy, and Cheryl Clarke embrace the mythic forms and characters in their poetry. Clarke, like Shange a decade before, has explored the many roads women take away from their ordained paths. In one poem, "living as a lesbian underground: a futuristic fantasy" (*Living As A Lesbian*) she creates lesbian as hero by casting her as a twenty-first-century resistance fighter. But her revolutionary is admonished to not ". . . get caught sleeping with/your shoes off/while women are forced back to the shelter/of homicidal husbands. . ." and above all to "Leave signs of struggle/Leave signs of triumph." (p.76) In *Experimental Love* Clarke has also published "living as a lesbian underground, ii." Here the escaping revolutionary is a writer, saving words and ideas from extinction. The act of revolution becomes a litany of familiar icons—Stevie Wonder, erotica, Pushkin—and ultimately a sexual act inciting the narrator to orgasm. The admonition here is that "memory is your only redemption." (p.9) In both poems Clarke insists on tying the past to the future and presenting women's global struggle as a triumph over the mundane horrors women face every day.

For me it is important that our mythic figures exist because ideas do affect experience and theory can affect practice. If we can create a root system, a path to our independent action from our internal and integral sources of power, we can make ourselves the center of our universe—if only in our fantasies. We can then change the way in which we view ourselves in this society.

The heroes and mythology that Black women create can be different from that which is currently familiar to us. The stories and poems we write that extol the leap women make from appendage to individual are grounded in the ordinary things that constitute all of our lives. And they are tied to a sense of community. This is the place where heroic change can begin. The surrealists believed that in order to change the world you had to first change your dreams. The women writers who develop characters of mythic proportions are doing just that. And the mythical stature emerges from their ability to link our survival as a people with the power of our humanity, rather than of brutal force.

Critics have often neglected to scrutinize fantasy or science fiction or place it within the context of literary and social constructs. But the genre, like any other popular art form, is very intimately related to the sensibilities of the broad-based populace. And poetry, despite its seeming exclusive academic position in contemporary society, is truly a populist oral art form and has provided a forum for rebellious voices for many social movements. Both genres offer a place for women to leave behind the social strictures that bind them to archaic roles. Where women have dared to create heroes in either fiction or poetry we can perceive a barometer of our secret fears and secret dreams. And we, as women, should be acutely aware of just how powerful dreams can be.

SELECTED BIBLIOGRAPHY

Baldwin, James. 1953. *Go Tell It on the Mountain*. New York: Dial Press.

Brooks, Gwendolyn. 1953. *Maud Martha*. New York: Harper and Row.

Burford, Barbara. 1989. *The Threshing Floor*. Ithaca, NY: Firebrand Books.

Butler, Octavia. 1979. *Kindred*. New York: Pocket Books.

Christian, Barbara. 1985. *Black Feminist Criticism*. New York: Pergamon Press.

Clarke, Cheryl. 1986. *Living As A Lesbian*. Ithaca, NY: Firebrand Books.

_____. 1993. *Experimental Love*. Ithaca, NY: Firebrand Books.

DeVeaux, Alexis. 1985. *Blue Heat*. Brooklyn, NY: Diva Publishing.

_____. 1981. *No*. Produced New York Henry St. Settlement.

Gearheart, Sally Miller. 1979. *Wanderground*. Boston: Alyson Publications.

Gomez, Jewelle. 1991. *The Gilda Stories*. Ithaca, NY: Firebrand Books.

Hernton, Calvin. 1987. *The Sexual Mountain and Black Women Writers*. New York: Doubleday.

Lorde, Audre. 1982. *Zami: A New Spelling of My Name*. Watertown, MA: Persephone Press.

McElroy, Colleen J. 1984. *Queen of the Ebony Isles*. Connecticut: Wesleyan University Press.

Morrison, Toni. 1977. *Song of Solomon*. New York: Alfred A. Knopf.

Parkerson, Michelle. 1983. *Waiting Rooms*. Washington, DC: Common Ground Press.

Piercy, Marge. 1976. *Woman on the Edge of Time*. New York: Alfred A. Knopf.

Van Sertima, Ivan. 1935. *Black Women in Antiquity*. New Brunswick, NJ: Transaction Books.

Shange, Ntozake. 1981. *For Colored Girls Who Have Considered Suicide When the Rainbow Is Enuf*. New York: Bantam Books.

Walker, Alice. 1973. *In Love and Trouble*. New York: Harcourt Brace Jovanovich.

_____. 1982. *The Color Purple*. New York: Harcourt Brace Jovanovich.

West, Dorothy. 1982 (reprint). *The Living Is Easy*. New York: Feminist Press.

IMAGINE A LESBIAN, A BLACK LESBIAN

Marianne Brown, me, and Sandra Lara (1991)
Photo: Michael Wakefield

Black women are still in the position of having to "imagine," discover and verify Black lesbian literature because so little has been written from an avowedly lesbian perspective. The near nonexistence of Black lesbian literature [which other Black lesbians and I do deeply feel] has everything to do with the politics of our lives, the total suppression of identity that all Black women, lesbian or not, must face.

Barbara Smith[1]

In the more than fifteen years since that statement appeared in Barbara Smith's article, "Toward a Black Feminist Criticism," much has changed in the literary arena for Black women writers, but too much has remained the same for Black lesbian writers and critics. While some attention has been given to the numbers of books published by Black women, little of the critical discussion has directly addressed the politics of publishing for Black women in general and Black lesbians specifically. Nor has it placed that work which does get published in a strong critical, literary context.

Sexuality has been raised as an issue in much of the recent analysis of such important writers as Toni Morrison and Alice Walker, yet it has consistently remained peripheral. Critics rarely address it as a substantial issue. Even the free-wheeling explicitness of Terry McMillan, or the sensual epics of Gloria Naylor, more often spark debates about male/female conflict rather than female sexuality or desire. Gender and sexuality have a profound effect on the quantity and quality of writing done by Black women (and concomitantly on that of other women of color in this country), and on the critical response to that work, as well as on the possibilities of publication.

It is specifically in the work of Black lesbian writers and critics that these two issues are unremittingly linked to themes and style. Yet many Black critical writers—feminist or not—still resist utilizing the expanded vision that Smith called for in discussing the work of Black women writers. I keep not finding myself within their analyses.

I.

The quality of light by which we scrutinize our
lives has direct bearing upon the product which

*we live, and upon the changes which we hope to
bring about through those lives.*

Audre Lorde[2]

Barbara Smith's demand for an alteration in the quality of
the light by which our lives and our work are examined is the
central focus of her initiation of the discussion of Black feminist
thought and its relationship to developing the art of critical writing
by and about Black women. For me, it was a trumpet, startling
and welcome. It was a call to take my own work seriously, to
take the work of other women and women of color seriously.
No longer were my poems and stories of consequence solely
within the context of a lesbian or a Black social circle. And my
work's value in one arena no longer meant inconsequence in
the other, or in the world at large. The basic principles of Black
feminist criticism as outlined by Smith are relatively elemen-
tary: a commitment to explore gender as well as racial politics; the assertion of a need to work from the assumption that
Black women's writing is part of an identifiable literary tradition; and acceptance of the importance of a search for a commonality of language and culture in the work of Black women.

These principles offer an expanded area of concentration
in which we can examine the work of African-American
women; and using one or all of the aspects Smith mentioned,
we can be naturally inclusive of the work of lesbians. What I
would add to Smith's groundbreaking essay is a more detailed
discussion of work by Black lesbian writers, something not possible earlier because of the (even greater) scarcity of material
in print. The primary work Smith examined was Toni Morrison's *Sula*. It is interesting to look at the lesbian bonds reflected
in ostensibly heterosexual works if only because it reveals just
how much of a lesbian subtext exists within the Black community despite attempts to conceal or deny it. But it is now cru-

cial to examine the work of out Black lesbian writers and discuss the many ways in which we approach the issues that affect us both as Black women and as lesbians. Such consideration assists me in assessing my own work and contributes to
the development of other Black lesbian writers and of Black
literature overall.

Smith's thesis set off a reactionary response from Black
critics quite out of proportion to the modest suggestions she
made. For many feminist critics years later—both heterosexual and lesbian, Black and white—race, not sex or gender, remains the predominant feature in any discussion of work by
women of color. It is, as Alice Walker said, "that perhaps white
women feminists, no less that white women generally, cannot
imagine black women have vaginas. Or if they can, where imagination leads them is too far to go."[3]

This observation was prompted by Patricia Meyer Spacks'
introduction to her book, *The Female Imagination*. In it Spacks
excuses the omission of African-American women with this statement: ". . . the books I talk about describe familiar experience,
belong to a familiar cultural setting; their particular immediacy
depends partly on these facts."[4] In one brief sentence she dis-
misses the value of the ability to live outside of ourselves when,
in fact, that ability is at the core of imagination and any true
liberation struggle. In that introduction the author admits to the
failure of her imagination when it comes to Black women. As
Alice Walker says, "Spacks never lived in nineteenth-century
Yorkshire, so why theorize about the Brontës?"[5]

Expanding historical discussion to include Black women
seems to stall some white feminist critics. In a parallel way, linking sexuality to race seems to make the interpretation of the
work of Black lesbians intimidating for Black critics. The lives
of "the other" are too remote, perhaps too explicit even for
those of us who think of ourselves as being in the vanguard

of change.

The question always hanging in the air around Black critics is: *Why do we have to talk about being lesbians in our work? Can't we just concentrate on the Black struggle?* It is disturbing to hear our work being dismissed by other Black feminist critics using terms such as *reductionist.* Hazel Carby, in her otherwise very useful book, *Reconstructing Womanhood,* poorly reconstructs Smith's call for an expansion of our critical perspective. She makes it sound as if Black lesbians are demanding that we each cordon off our specific areas of interest and not venture outside of them. Smith's message is not that looking at literature with a Black feminist eye reduces "the experience of all black women to a common denominator and [limits] black feminist critics to an exposition of an equivalent black female imagination,"[6] as Carby presumes. The idea is rather that such a perspective adds a layer of information and experience from which all critics, lesbian or not, would benefit.

It is the explicitly lesbian nature of Smith's discussion which sends many Black feminist critics scuttling backward. Asking feminist critics (Black or white) to express solidarity with a lesbian vision is asking them to also question their accommodation to the status quo (or the patriarchy, to use an unfashionable term) in order to succeed. Because a great many of the Black women critics being published today have academia rather than community activism as their base of legitimacy, lesbianism may be an aspect of our culture they can't afford to identify with professionally.

One example of such distancing occurred in 1987 when Rutgers University held a conference called "Changing Our Own Words." The two-day event featured presentations by almost every major critic of Black women's work in print—Hazel Carby, Hortense J. Spillers, Mary Helen Washington, Claudia Tate, Deborah McDowell, Houston Baker among them. Although Barbara Smith's article was a reference for several of the speakers, no lesbian critics spoke on the program. (There were several of us in the audience.) The two critics—Carby and Baker—who addressed work with explicit lesbian content (the film of Alice Walker's *The Color Purple,* and *Sassafras, Cypress and Indigo,* a novel by Ntozake Shange) never mentioned the word *lesbian* nor the importance of the lesbian perspective. When questioned at the end of the sessions neither speaker could rationally explain why. Each essentially said that the lesbian content was not significant or germane to their discussion. In works with interpersonal relationships at their core, the relevance of the form of those relationships seems obvious.

Some critical essayists such as Calvin Hernton, Alice Walker, and Barbara Christian[7] have not fallen into this sin of omission, but for many feminist critics (white as well as Black), the work of lesbian writers remains foreign territory they see little advantage in exploring. For all African-Americans, female and male, who were forbidden by law the right to read, politics can never be separated from our literary tradition. For women who have been so callously forbidden the right to control our own bodies, the issues of sexuality and gender are equally intrinsic to the discussion of our work. For Black lesbians, and all women of color who are lesbians and whose frame of reference is colonialism, the inclusion of both perspectives is even more critical given the historical position of nonwhite women in this country. I cannot afford to overlook the full spectrum of work created by writers—the writing of Hazel Carby or Patricia Meyer Spacks has the potential to inform what all of us write. But I do not rely on critics to offer me legitimacy, especially when they insist on my invisibility. I must continue to move toward a Black feminist criticism. The three points of reference that Smith defines in her article serve as an important jumping off point for me.

II.

Within the celebration of the erotic in all our en-
deavors, my work becomes a conscious decision,
a longed-for bed which I enter gratefully and from
which I rise up empowered.

Audre Lorde[8]

We must continue to insist that being a lesbian is larger than simply what we do in bed, that it has pervasive social and political implications. But it *is* what we do in bed, or that our identity depends on what we do in bed, that presents a sticking point for critics. This is more than simply homophobia. It is, as Amber Hollibaugh termed it, "erotophobia"[9]—fear of anything pertaining to the erotic or desire, especially connected with women. The fear is a part of the deeply puritanical roots of this country, as well as the response of oppressed people of color, and women, whose identities have often been reduced simply to sexual functions. This erotophobia seems to be at the heart of Black feminist critics' inability to address the work of lesbians and Black lesbians within the Black literary context. Even where sexuality is not a predominant or central element, the work of Black lesbian writers may be presumed to be explicit. And in work where sexuality is explicit or directly implied (as in *The Color Purple*), it is ignored.

"Miss Esther's Land," a story by Barbara Banks published in *Home Girls,* captures an essence of Black lesbian life and writing. It is full of the cultural references of Black life, and strongly articulates the perceptions of Black women through the eyes of Black lesbians in rural circumstances. It is a fine example of a wholistic view of Black women's lives, a view that cannot dismiss the questions of either race or sexuality. And because it is particularly well written, this story provides the opportunity to discuss the fullness of writing by Black women.

"Miss Esther's Land" tells of an enduring lesbian relationship as recounted by one of the partners as she nears her last days. On her seventy-fifth birthday, Esther must decide between leaving her land to her lover of forty years, Molly, or doing as Molly would prefer and deeding it to the Black townspeople who want to design a new community. Within a few pages Banks raises a wide range of interlocking concerns. Esther must confront what her obsessive love of her land has meant to her relationship with both Molly and the townspeople, Black and white. Shown from her perspective, Esther's sense of preservation is natural—the land is a powerful symbol of freedom. She is a farm woman who remembers her grandfather, an ex-slave, and his toil to work the land. But to the townspeople and to Molly, who has been their school teacher and champion, the acreage is more than a pastoral monument to their history: it is a seed for the future, one only Esther can secure.

Within this layered context, Banks reveals the subtle issues Molly and Esther face. Leaving the land to Molly in her will is not safe. Molly is not blood relation, her status as lover/partner is undefined within the Black community. Their union is accepted but unacknowledged publicly. The Black community has a desperate interest in the land: whites will not let them develop their section of town to provide services and suitable homes. This land offers them the chance to take control of their own lives for the first time since slavery. And Esther's son, who does not take the long view, would have little difficulty retrieving the bequested land from Molly in court and delivering it into the hands of white land developers for the highest price. Esther, living at the edge of the intruding Route 60 and searching herself for the meaning of the sudden death of her ancient apple tree, can only feel sorrow that everyone else does not love her farm as she does—for its memories.

The crucial subtext of her dilemma is that she and Molly are lovers. Their physical relationship is made clear by Esther's recollection of their first days together:

> Esther kissed her. She pressed her mouth softly upon Molly's and was struck still by the newness of the thing, by her own naiveté. She did not know how to touch her, was not sure if she should, was afraid she'd spoil this wonderful thing by making it carnal.
> Frustrated she stammered, "Now what do I do?" By morning, the issue had been resolved.[10]

Molly and Esther relate physically in an easy way. Their sexuality is not a source of guilt for them, but rather one of joy. Yet they are aware of the social dangers such a relationship presents. On the day of Esther's seventy-fifth birthday, Molly removes her things from their bedroom to a guest room, a task obviously repeated many times during their four decades together. Presumably this allays the suspicions of the family visiting for the celebration; it at least provides a way for those who are suspicious to dismiss their misgivings. Yet, even as she packs her things, Molly says to Esther, "What makes you think they don't know anyway? If anyone of them has ever thought about it, they know. But people are wonderful at ignoring things when it's to their advantage. . . ."[11]

In these few pages Barbara Banks tells us much about what it might really be like to have a relationship with another woman in a Black rural community. It is also emblematic of the position in which Black lesbians find ourselves within the Black and the feminist literary communities: our sexual lives remain unacknowledged, (as were Celie and Shug's at the Rutgers conference), yet those same sexual lives are a solid wall blocking out full consideration of our work and existence.

Banks' story begins exploring the strength of family by portraying one of the classic attitudes to lesbianism in the Black community without forgetting the historical perspective. It is the analysis of lesbian works like this that opens up the meaning of race and sex in our society.

Her, written by Cherry Muhanji, is a novel to similarly consider. It is a lyrical narrative about life on a block in Detroit in the 1950s and '60s. While the main action of the novel is not explicitly lesbian, the underpinnings certainly are. A young girl, Sunshine, is brought home by her boyfriend to live in his mother's house, where an assortment of sisters and aunts and uncles up from the South also live. Accustomed to bearing the scorn of other Black women because of her exceptionally fair skin, the girl is sullen and uncommunicative. She mistrusts the friendship offered by her mother-in-law, Charlotte, since she's unused to the gruff interchange that is common in a house full of working-class Black women. She cannot find her voice, or even her own name.

Sunshine flees this family and moves in with Mrs. Ricky Wintergreen, a notorious and mysterious owner of a local night club. Sunshine takes the name Kali and remakes herself in the image of Mrs. Wintergreen. But in finding a new persona she also finds herself under the dangerous influence of a psychotic pimp. The neighborhood and its characters represent a full cross section of a very dynamic world, much like the one I grew up in: pimps, prostitutes, white hustlers living in close proximity to people working as maids, Pullman porters, hairdressers —with the gay characters easily distributed on either side of the law. It is an interdependent neighborhood that has yet to devolve into the urban isolation characteristic of the '70s and '80s.

Wintergreen, as she is called reverently by the patrons of her club where she sings, is an enigma. We learn that the subtle tension that resonates on the block between her and Charlotte exists because they had been lovers during the war years. The tragedy comes not from their desire but from their failure to have fulfilled themselves. But Kali's potential tragedy draws them back to each other, shaking the foundation of the lives they've built separately. Meeting Wintergreen up close for the first time in years Charlotte sees the dramatic damage that has been done to her feet during the war. With little hesitation, "Charlotte planted tiny kisses along the high and low places of the broken feet, washing them with great tears."[12]

The expression of their love is so powerful it draws Charlotte's husband to the door of the room. "For the first time he saw that his wife was capable of deep feeling. And that discovery moved him in ways that he couldn't articulate then . . . The only thing he heard was the name Ricky repeated over and over again. He removed his head from the parlor door and shut it quietly."[13] Ricky Wintergreen bridges the years and lives between them: "Gently she brought Charlotte's head close and kissed her mouth. After the first lingering taste, Ricky pushed her tongue inside Charlotte's mouth and stayed."[14] When their desire can be met fully, a circle is completed and action can be taken. Their reunion is at the heart of the community of women who rescue Kali.

Muhanji is able to draw the picture of lesbian love within the context of a Black community without sacrificing the integrity of either reality. The mingled working class/underclass roots of her story represent a world I feel a kinship with. Use of that historic period allows Muhanji to capture a moment in our history before Black innocence is completely lost, when the mythology surrounding one character, Wintergreen, can carry a community forward to action. Economic survival, community integrity, and desire are at the heart of Muhanji's characters just as they are for Banks'.

The strongest writing by Black lesbians reflects these multiple concerns. It examines how Black lesbians survived within the context of the legacy of slavery and racism and utilizes the complex nature of social and sexual interactions to reflect society at large. The development of methods of absorbing or ignoring differences within the African-American community; the contrast between the response to homosexuality by the traditional Black working poor and that of the striving, Black middle class; the flowering of gay life in the Black community that lived outside of the law; the difference between Black urban and Black rural lesbian life—all are areas of study that aid in expanding the Black feminist vision.

III.

At the same time that I emphasize the recognition of the specifics of racial and sexual politics I also suggest, as Smith does, that no work be considered without placing it within some additional literary context. In her book, *How to Suppress Women's Writing*,[15] Joanna Russ catalogues a number of insidious practices for dismissing women's literature. Isolation, Russ points out, has been a chief method in the critical establishment and it is manifested in many different ways. Many feminist critics and historians have been guilty of using isolation against the work of Black women and Black lesbians.

As a writer of fantasy fiction, I am always pushing doubly hard to have my work seen within the context of other fantasy writing. Because I am Black and a lesbian, critics of the genre don't quite know where to place a Black lesbian vampire novel. And many feminist critics don't have the background in genre fiction that would allow them to place the work in a context (Susanna Sturgis, who reviewed my novel in *Feminist Bookstore News,* and Patricia Roth Schwartz in *Sojourner* were two exceptions). Reviewers for African-American publications ignored the book completely, as if mystified by a complexity of vision.

A narrowness, similar to that which plagues science fiction critics, has also afflicted me at times. When looking at comic fiction I have found it difficult to appreciate, or even recognize, humor on the printed page. Several times in past articles I've discussed Ann Allen Shockley's novel, *Say Jesus and Come to Me.*[16] Shockley (the author of *Loving Her,* the first explicit and sympathetic novel about a Black lesbian, published in 1974), drew on a short story she'd written earlier to describe the life of a Black preacher, Reverend Myrtle Black. Lust and ambition seem to drive her from one pastorate to the next seeking new converts, new conquests, and power. That is until she meets Travis Lee, a soul singer who's recently repented her sins and been born again. As it stands, this work presents problems for me. Its transitions feel too abrupt. It ignores the patently homophobic stance of most Fundamentalist Christian dogma. The core of Rev. Black's political campaign is feminism at its most self-absorbed—a difficult point to overcome if we're to sympathize with the reverend.

Yet as someone pointed out to me sometime after I had read and reviewed the book, *Say Jesus and Come to Me* may work for many people as that rare form: comic fiction. Perhaps because I, like others who feel they are in an embattled community, have needed each piece of literature to represent the best of all that I feel and believe, I had been unable to see its comic possibilities and the value of that genre. I had not looked at it in relationship to the comic sketches of Alice Childress or the bawdy humor of comedian Jackie Moms Mabley. In light of those traditions it makes sense that Rev. Black's licentious spirit and Travis' miraculous conversion take on such melodramatic proportions rather than the more mundane framework I anticipated. I realized that I had not considered Shockley's work fully to assess the value within the comic genre, much as other critics have neglected placing my novel within the context of vampire fiction or African-American historical fiction. Ignoring the cultural or literary context is another way of isolating our work and denying it the critical attention it deserves.

Another form of isolation, even within the appropriate cultural or literary context, grows out of the fear some feminist critics seem to have of raising questions about the quality of the writing of Black women. Linda Powell pointed out in *Conditions* magazine that ". . . if a black woman speaks the language and is nice around white folks . . . she can speak at conferences. She can write reviews. And even if she's mediocre it's not bad for a negro."[17] It falls to Black feminist and lesbian critics to explore the crucial issues of literary quality even if others will not. And by literary quality I do not mean adherence to traditional forms or content, but rather how well a writer uses her own language to achieve her goals within the piece being examined.

My work may be isolated by not being addressed within the genre where it might rightfully belong but more importantly, it is isolated, and the development of my craft is impeded, by not being discussed professionally as well as politically. This lack of serious consideration on the part of magazine and anthology editors may come simply from a shortage of time and money, or even skills. But often it is attributable to the low expectations editors have for the work of women, and women of color in particular. As a response I've come to rely on a circle of writers/editors whom I trust to be tough, to question what I don't know and what they don't know, so that my writing, even where flawed, represents a sincere effort to communicate, not simply time spent at a typewriter.

Another method of isolation is that of offering up one Black lesbian writer as the spokeswoman and the authority and ignoring the work of others. Black feminist critics seem to have fallen into this error as easily as others. At any African-American literary gathering, if the question of Black lesbians is raised, Audre Lorde's name is offered as the token. Certainly Lorde is the most well-known out Black lesbian writer, but what of Cheryl Clarke, Alexis DeVeaux, Terri Jewell, Michelle Cliff, Sapphire, Kate Rushin, Angela Bowen, Lindajean Brown, and the many more who have been publishing for the past fifteen years?

It was Audre, herself, who made me most aware of this issue when I called to ask if I could interview her for the film, *Before Stonewall.* Her response was to ask if she were the only Black lesbian in the film. She did not want white audiences to use her to feel satisfied, as if having seen her they'd seen all Black lesbians. To avoid this Audre suggested the inclusion of another of her contemporaries, Muaua Flowers. The result is a lively discussion between friends who are relating their experiences rather than a singular Black spokesperson.

Unfortunately, the same tokenizing tactic is used by Black feminist critics as well. For them to rely on knowing the work of one Black lesbian, or two, effectively stunts the growth of other Black lesbian writers and renders them invisible. In preparing this work it was possible to locate full-length works by a larger number of Black lesbians than was possible when "Toward a Black Feminist Criticism" was originally published. Some of these writers, such as Audre Lorde, are already quite well-known to us, and my goal is to expand our critical field of reference. Discussing the work of little-known writers, such as Cherry Muhanji and Barbara Banks, along with the standard-bearers, helps enrich the field. This is in opposition to the prevailing concept behind commercial presses: *We have one already.* A philosophy like this leaves individual Black lesbian writers with too much responsibility and not enough room to create. Imagine a publisher saying: We have enough white male writers from the East Coast this year. Let's not bother with those submissions. And why don't we just skip that new Norman Mailer book.

IV.

Language—however we adapt it or adapt to it—is eternally political, because language reveals to what degree the writer accepts or rejects the prevailing culture.

Cheryl Clarke[18]

My attempt to break through these forms of isolation and place my work within the appropriate tradition is an acknowledgment of the value of Black women's use of our own language and cultural experience. Some feminists emphasize the idea that *We can do anything men can do.* Women can hold nontraditional jobs, maintain a corporate image, sound and act as aggressively as a man. This is much the same type of message delivered to Blacks by civil rights leaders—show white people we were just like them. But another equally important aspect of feminism is the exploration of things that are not the same as men, that are more particular to women: crafts, music, religions, ways of processing information.

For Black women writers whose language and inflection, as well as interpretation of cultural experiences, are a complex amalgam of European-American and African or Caribbean influences, the acknowledgment of difference is central to liberation and to writing. Questions about narrative voice, dialects, occupations and preoccupations certainly yield revealing information when raised about the work of Black lesbian writers. In 1992 the American Family Association excerpted the work of Black lesbian poet, Sapphire, in an attempt to stir up controversy about the funding of *The Portable Lower East Side,* a New York magazine.[19] Taking her work out of context AFA attempted to show that she was supporting "wilding" or gang rape, when in fact her poem was an attempt to step inside the minds and hearts of the boys who perpetrated the Central Park jogger rape. While I expect the Religious Right to deliberately misread our language and perspective, I always hope that Black feminist critics will not make that error. I wondered where they were as this Black writer was vilified in the national press.

Critics must be able to admit when our experience or sensibilities are limited and do not allow us the openness to analyze material that is outside our definitions. We then have to do the work to be open and to learn. To demand academic language, or classical European-American references or structure, is to deny the voice of Black women. For many, my entire discussion may be discounted if my choice of references is drawn from short story writers and novelists and poets equally; or if they are drawn from lesbian literary presses and placed right alongside university or commercial presses unapologetically. To be prejudiced against that mix ignores the political considerations that influence who has access to publication and who does not. In examining the voice of Black lesbians it is the element of difference which often alienates Black feminist critics. It is more valuable to embrace that difference, whether comfortable or not, and learn from it.

V.

I am trying to point out that lesbian-feminism has the potential of reversing and transforming a major component in the system of women's oppression. . . . If radical lesbian-feminism purports an anti-racist, anti-classist, anti-woman-hating vision of bonding. . . then all people struggling to transform the character of relationships in this culture have something to learn from lesbians.

Cheryl Clarke[20]

The articulation of guiding principles and the practice of them is not "from my mouth to God," as my Aunt Irene says. A major stumbling block for me is that 90 percent of the time when I'm asked to write about the work of another Black woman, the review or article is being requested for a white and often straight publication. My reticence to write something which will be perceived as negative about a Black woman or Black lesbian in a mainstream journal (no matter how "constructively critical" it might be) is as hard as a plaster cast. The discussion among several Black women critics (myself included) that I mentioned earlier was published in *Conditions: Nine*. Some readers who felt our remarks were too critical of established Black lesbian writers cancelled subscriptions or harangued us personally for publishing such work and in a "white" publication (although the magazine's editorial collective had a substantial representation of women of color). Some protesters, Black and white, appeared to feel that the work of Black lesbians is too delicate to withstand close examination. If one is able to see our work within the context of years of tradition, both written and oral, that assumption is absurd.

I do believe that we have much to learn from each other's

work but still, like those who criticized our contribution to *Conditions: Nine,* I can't dismiss the racism and homophobia that has operated within progressive journals of all kinds. This means that my choice of words has a softer edge when discussing a Black woman whose work does not satisfy me, or that I avoid discussion of another Black lesbian writer altogether. Still it is important for me to speak so that I do not succumb to the same alienation I find inexcusable in others. It's crucial that all writers interested in serious critical work acknowledge our limitations and, rather than resigning ourselves to alienation or ignorance, begin to bridge the gaps that separate us from new experiences.

I find the principles of Black feminist criticism offer me the broadest perspective so that this loss or exclusion does not occur. I'm not at all interested in assessing, dismissing, or promoting one particular genre, school, or writer. Nor do I advocate censoring out what might be considered "incorrect" for the Black image or the Black lesbian image and supporting only idealized, sanitized images. I'm more interested in the personal and literary chances that Black women take and how we can surprise and sometimes delight each other.

For me, feminist criticism must encompass that place where philosophy and activism intersect. The quality of life and work must be defined by principles that may seem academic on paper but are vital points of reference in our lives, and starting places for action. While some critics may be able to avoid examination of the discomforting space between thought and action, there are also many who will not want to. Black lesbian feminist writers have little choice.

I began this discussion by exploring what has not been done. But I continue to believe that there is a lot that can be done, and that the effort benefits all writers. Now, as was always true, recognizing these possibilities does require a great deal of realignment of how we think, feel, and react. The first step is, as always, imagination.

NOTES

1. Barbara Smith, "Toward a Black Feminist Criticism," *Conditions: Two* (1977), 39.

2. Audre Lorde, "Poetry Is Not a Luxury," in *Sister Outsider* (Trumansburg, NY: The Crossing Press, 1984), 36.

3. Alice Walker, "One Child of One's Own," in *In Search of Our Mothers' Gardens* (New York: Harcourt Brace Jovanovich, 1983), 373.

4. Ibid., 372.

5. Ibid., 373.

6. Hazel V. Carby, *Reconstructing Womanhood* (New York: Oxford University Press, 1987), 10.

7. Calvin Hernton, *The Sexual Mountain and Black Women Writers* (New York: Doubleday, 1989); Alice Walker, *In Search of Our Mothers' Gardens;* Barbara Christian, *Black Feminist Criticism* (New York: Pergamon Press, 1985).

8. Audre Lorde, "Uses of the Erotic," in *Sister Outsider,* 55.

9. Amber Hollibaugh, "The Erotophobic Voice of Women," *New York Native,* No. 7, September 25, 1983, 33.

10. Barbara Banks, "Miss Esther's Land", in *Home Girls: A Black Feminist Anthology,* edited by Barbara Smith (New York: Kitchen Table: Women of Color Press, 1983), 185.

11. Ibid., 194.

12. Cherry Muhanji, *Her* (San Francisco: Aunt Lute Foundation, 1990), 156.

13. Ibid., 157.

14. Ibid., 158.

15. Joanna Russ, *How to Suppress Women's Writing* (Austin: University of Texas Press, 1983).

16. Ann Allen Shockley, *Say Jesus and Come to Me* (New York: Avon Books, 1982).

17. Cheryl Clarke, Jewelle Gomez, Evelynn Hammonds, Bonnie Johnson, Linda Powell, "Black Women on Black Women Writers," *Conditions: Nine* (1983), 101.

18. Cheryl Clarke, review of *Nappy Edges* by Ntozake Shange, *Conditions: Five* (1979), 160.

19. Sapphire, "Wild Thing," *The Portable Lower East Side: Queer City,* Vol. 8, No. 2 (1991), 41.

20. Cheryl Clarke, "Lesbianism: An Act of Resistance," in *This Bridge Called My Back,* edited by Cherríe Moraga and Gloria Anzaldúa (New York: Kitchen Table: Women of Color Press, 1983), 134.

LORRAINE HANSBERRY:

Uncommon Warrior

Faculty and staff of the Loft Film and Theater Center (1973)

I was born on the South Side of Chicago. I was born black and female. I was born in a depression after one world war, and came into my adolescence during another. While I was still in my teens the first atom bombs were dropped on human beings at Nagasaki and Hiroshima. And by the time I was twenty-three years old, my government and that of the Soviet Union had entered actively into the worst conflict of nerves in human history—the Cold War. . .I have, like all of you, on a thousand occasions seen indescribable displays of

> *man's very real inhumanity to man, and I have*
> *come to maturity, as we all must, knowing that*
> *greed and malice and indifference to human mis-*
> *ery and bigotry and corruption, brutality, and per-*
> *haps above all else, ignorance—the prime ancient*
> *and persistent enemy of man—abound in this*
> *world. I say all of this to say that one cannot live*
> *with sighted eyes and feeling heart and not know*
> *and react to the miseries which afflict this*
> *world.. .*[1]

These words, from a speech Lorraine Hansberry made to a Black writers' conference in New York City in 1959, could have easily been my own, or those of others whom I know and work with. What is most familiar is the sense of disbelief at what we, as human beings, will do to each other, in the name of humanity.

These words provide a welcome opportunity to rediscover the depth and breadth of Hansberry's social and political concerns, to see how they are manifest in her work. Today one need only say *Raisin,* and the world of her play, *A Raisin in the Sun,* springs fully realized to my mind. It's easy, now, to recall that she was the first Black woman playwright to be produced on Broadway and the youngest ever to win the New York Critics Circle Award. When I saw the film of her play starring Sidney Poitier, Claudia McNeil, Ruby Dee, and Diana Sands, I felt a new world open up to me. Not simply that she was a Black woman writer who'd been recognized by her profession but because her ideas resonated so deeply inside me and had not been raised in film before. To a young Black woman with writing aspirations Hansberry's emergence was a miracle then. She has since entered our collective consciousness. And in some ways that casual acceptance of her accomplishments diminishes the impact of those achievements and their lasting value in our lives today.

I say *rediscover* because she was proud of being "young, gifted and Black" at a time when Black women were thought to be merely long-suffering matriarchs with sharp tongues. Her pride is the key to the uncommon consciousness of this woman. She was truly capable of being a warrior in what Barbara Smith has termed "the most expansive of revolutions."[2] This revolution resists the idea that "one for all and all for me" is a workable attitude. This revolution can no longer focus solely on the wrongs of the past as experienced by one group. Such a narrow stance leaves too much room for us to solve our problems and then perpetuate misdeeds against some other group.

As a warrior in this expansive revolution, Hansberry realized that all acts of violence are connected; and she did not feel so insecure that the freedom of others frightened her. In fact, she understood that our personal will, our fears, our joys, would often be in conflict with our social and political responsibility. She was prepared to explore her own insecurities and prejudices in order to confront the larger issues, to confront that system of thinking that had held Black people in subjugation long after slavery was abolished.

In rediscovering this warrior waging this expansive revolution, I reclaim her as my own. Like all of us she was more than a snapshot or a bibliography. The legacy she left is not only that of a Black writer but also that of a political activist and a Black woman. I need her desperately, and so should we all.

In the early 1900s, the actor, singer, and minstrel Bert Williams made famous a song entitled, "Nobody." Although it's clear that the white theatre establishment thought this an accurate description of Blacks, Bert Williams did not. He said, "It is no disgrace to be a Negro, but it is very inconvenient."[3] From nineteenth-century melodramas and minstrel shows to the

1920s musicals like *Shuffle Along,* Black shows delivered deliberately constructed messages: Blacks are harmless, not always happy, but definitely as American as pizza pie. While theatres like the Lafayette lit up Harlem in the 1920s with Black stars such as Florence Mills and Charles Gilpin, white audiences were still intrigued by Ethel Barrymore in blackface and O'Neill's rendition of the Black experience in *The Emperor Jones.*

Many musicals which originated in Harlem were moved downtown to the big time, making the Depression years one of the largest periods of employment of Black artists on Broadway. The country wanted singing and dancing even when it couldn't afford food. Musicals and melodramas became even more popular with whites, as well as with Blacks, during World War II.

Although the kindest thing that used to be said about the 1950s is that "nothing happened," that, in fact, was not true. At the beginning of that decade, the most well-known Black dramatic character was still the mammy figure embodied by Ethel Waters in *Member of the Wedding,* which opened on Broadway in 1950. Langston Hughes was adapting his tales of Semple for the stage; veteran Black actor Canada Lee had just died; and his pal, Sidney Poitier, was working toward his own stardom while running a rib joint on Seventh Avenue and 131st Street.

Outside the theatre, in the daylight, things were not much brighter. But things were happening. Segregation in public schools was being challenged in the courts; citizens were being hauled before the House Un-American Activities Committee (HUAC), which tried to intimidate them into betraying their principles and their friends; Japanese-Americans were still trying to rebuild their lives after being released from American internment camps in the Midwest; and, as Hansberry noted, the Cold War was casting a chilly pall over everything.

It was into this broad arena of change that Lorraine Hansberry stepped. She arrived as an outsider, removed from the hurly-burly of Harlem, but certainly not unaware of it. Born in 1930, she was accustomed to seeing the great thinkers of the day such as W.E.B. DuBois as visitors to her childhood home. Her family had lived through the integration of a white neighborhood, and her father invested a good bit of his time and professional expertise (both financial and legal) winning them the right to live anywhere in Chicago that they chose.

As a writer Hansberry was, although an outsider, truly a descendant of the New York City writers who came before her. She'd steeped herself in drama from the age of fourteen. She saw as much kinship with the Irish playwrights, such as Synge and O'Casey, as with Langston Hughes. She understood the real element of truth in the tired axiom that "people are just people." She saw that in order for a great work to be genuinely universal it had to be painfully specific. The truth of Black lives had to be explored, not recast into imitations of white life, before Black theatre would take its place in world drama. While the beginning of the 1950s saw the revival of the 1921 musical hit, *Shuffle Along,* the end of the decade witnessed a questioning of this simplistic acceptance of one-dimensional Black characters who existed only in relationship to the white world.

What happens to a dream deferred?
  Does it dry up
  like a raisin in the sun?
  or fester like a sore—
  and then run?
Does it stink like rotten meat?
Or crust and sugar over—

like a syrupy sweet
Maybe it just sags
like a heavy load.
Or does it explode?[4]

These questions posed by Langston Hughes were the same ones that Lorraine Hansberry began to address in her play, *A Raisin in the Sun,* which opened at the Barrymore Theatre in 1959. Hansberry wanted to explore the specifics of Black life that went deeper than the grinning image white audiences found palatable. She was addressing the ideas and urges that fueled our lives politically and personally. She began in a small room, examining it in detail, looking for the universal truth of dignity:

> *The Younger living room would be a comfortable and well-ordered room if it were not for a number of indestructible contradictions to this state of being. Its furnishings are typical and undistinguished and their primary feature now is that they have clearly had to accommodate the living of too many people for too many years and they are tired.... Weariness has, in fact, won in this room. Everything has been polished, washed, sat on, used, scrubbed too often. All pretenses but living itself have long since vanished from the very atmosphere of this room.*[5]

She began in a small room with the simple story of a working-class family trying to move into a better neighborhood. The family, much like her own in spirit, became a symbol of our aspirations. But as a writer, Hansberry's work is even bigger than that. She arrived at a pivotal point in the development of Black drama and Black thinking. She believed, as others like Alice Childress and Louis Peterson were beginning to, in probing the specifics of her characters by peeling back the generalities, whether those generalities were culture, ethnicity, gender, or language. She was convinced that beneath any combination of these elements was a distinct human being who, given a voice, would make a valid statement about humankind.

In addition to opening up questions about the validity of middle-class aspirations, *Raisin* also raised other primary issues: the right of women to control our own bodies and our intellectual independence, the conservatism of the underclasses, the myth of the Black matriarch, the connection between Africans and African-Americans—topics not generally being raised by Blacks in public. In the 1960s, some Black Nationalist activists suggested Hansberry was an inadequate spokesperson for the Black revolution by saying she was "too middle class." Those who made this observation mistakenly assumed that socioeconomic status and personality are as immutable as race. They also ignored the fact that many major male social revolutionaries have risen from the middle classes: Ghandi, Marx, Ho Chi Minh, Nkrumah, Castro, King.

Hansberry was able to create substantial characters who lived and grew. The Younger family—each character, individually, and the whole—symbolized the opposing systems of thought that continue to tear this country apart. It was not just a matter of Mama's nurturant dream of a house versus Walter Lee's entrepreneurial dream of a liquor store. The contest was also between the individual and the collective good. This was *not* simply a play about upward mobility.

Just as the subtleties of her play have been overlooked, many critics have neglected the full ramifications of Hansberry's life as a cultural worker. Her plays, the product of a young and diligent mind, work dramaturgically within the context of the drama of her day. At the time she arrived, American theatre had fallen head-first into the pit of naturalism, reducing plays from poetry to newspaper clippings. She was working in one medium (playwriting) which was taking its shape from another (fiction writing), and it was doing so poorly. Drama left the realm of wonder where it had begun, the church and ritual which was its birthplace. It moved into an undefined arena filling its artists with self-consciousness about their craft. The best known, such as Eugene O'Neill or Carson McCullers, sought expression through faithful or poetic presentations of "reality" rather than exploring the tradition of the transportation of the heart and soul. Hansberry took the naturalistic style and infused it with comprehensive ideas in ways that other writers writing about Black characters were not doing. Beyond the message that Black is normal and good, there was no other dimension to the political and social concepts of Black drama. From her earliest work to her unfinished novel her writing reveals that Hansberry was an intensely political person. That politic embraced the totality of who Black people were in this country.

Once she was proclaimed the reigning queen of Black drama by critics, Hansberry did not let up. In her next play, *The Sign in Sidney Brustein's Window* (1964), she had the audacity to make the central characters white. The play's production was met with scorn from both white and Black critics, in spite of the fact that white people had been describing and defining Black people for centuries, both on paper and in real life. Although that play also included a gay male character, people were not interested in talking about him at all, much less in examining Hansberry's reasons for his inclusion.

Lorraine Hansberry had many stories to tell. She did not feel the need to justify any one of them. She had strong concern for a variety of issues affecting this society and did not cower in the shadow of 1950s political repression. Hansberry flew to a Peace Congress in Uruguay in 1957 to deliver a speech in place of Paul Robeson, whose passport had been revoked by the United States because of his leftist organizing. When she returned to the United States the government revoked her passport .

Also in 1957, after the Mattachine Society's Harry Hay (the leader of the first gay male organization) had already been called before the HUAC along with a number of "suspected" homosexuals, Hansberry continued to publicly espouse human rights. In that same period she wrote a letter to *The Ladder,* the first journal published for lesbians in this country. In it, she said:

> *It is time that "half the human race" had something to say about the nature of its existence. . . In this kind of work there may be women to emerge who will be able to formulate a new and possible concept that homosexual persecution and condemnation has at its roots not only social ignorance but a philosophically active anti-feminist dogma. .* [6]

Anticipating the modern feminist movement, she wrote in an unpublished manuscript in 1957:

> *Woman, like the Negro, like the Jew, like colonial peoples, even in ignorance, is incapable of accepting the role with harmony. This is because it is an unnatural role. The station of woman is hardly one that she would assume by choice, any more than men would. It must necessarily be imposed on her by force. . .A status not freely chosen or entered into by an individual or group is necessarily one of oppression and the oppressed are by their nature. . .forever in ferment and agitation against their condition and what they understand to be their oppressors. If not by overt rebellion or*

*revolution, then in the thousand and one ways they
will devise with and without consciousness to al-
ter their condition.*[7]

Because Hansberry has been regarded only within the
context of Black (mostly male) dramatists, her position as a
woman has been ignored. Discussion of *Raisin* is centered most
often around Walter Lee and his frustrations, or his conflict with
his mother. The character frequently overlooked is Beneatha,
Walter Lee's sister, and the most autobiographical of Hansberry's characters.

Early in the play, Beneatha has this exchange with the African who is pushing her to marry him:

> *Beneatha: "You never understood that there is
> more than one kind of feeling which can exist be-
> tween a man and a woman—or at least, there
> should be."*
>
> *Asagai shakes his head gently: "No, between
> a man and a woman there need be only one kind
> of feeling. I have that for you . . ."*
>
> *Beneatha: "I know—and by itself—it won't
> do. I can find that anywhere."*
>
> *Asagai: "For a woman it should be enough."*
>
> *Beneatha: "I know because that's what it
> says in all the novels that men write. But it
> isn't . . ."*[8]

These words were not put in the mouth of Walter Lee's sister merely to show her up as rebellious and troublesome: they
were Lorraine Hansberry's political beliefs. In some unpublished notes she examines the idea that "feminine" traits, such
as love, compassion, and understanding are reserved only for
woman's personality. She wrote:

*This is the supreme insult against men. Is it only
woman who truly possesses the most magnificent
features of the human race—I, a woman, think
not—and it is time men decided it is the great
slander of the ages—to take our hands—truly—
as comrades.*[9]

She understood clearly the nature of relationships between
women and men, and just as sharply she saw the relationships
between nations. She foresaw that the betrayal of the Cuban
Revolution would come from the U.S. government, not from
Fidel Castro, and she said so in the *New York Times*.[10] She recognized that colonialism was breaking the backs of people of
color not unlike herself and articulated this in her play *Les Blancs*,
which she began writing in 1960. She was in tune with Zora
Neale Hurston's comment that Black women are "the mules
of the world," and she refused to be one, saying so every opportunity she had.

Because we have studied Hansberry only as a dramatist
and not as a cultural worker and thinker, we have lost touch
with the urgency of her political message and the poetry of her
writing, in particular her prose. In an essay for Broadway's *Playbill* magazine she wrote:

*I remember being startled when I first saw my
grandmother rocking away on her porch. All my
life I had heard that she was a great beauty and
no one had ever remarked that they meant a half
century before. The woman I met was as wrinkled
as a prune and could hardly hear and barely see
and always seemed to be thinking of other times.
But she could still rock and talk and even made
wonderful cupcakes which were like cornbread*

only sweet. She died the next summer and that is
all that I remember about her, except that she was
born in slavery and had memories of it and they
didn't sound anything like Gone With the Wind.[11]

Just as her grandmother's memories were able to shed light on the past and reshape her thinking about the Black reality, Hansberry is able to look again at our lives as women and shine a light on them so we remember what it was really supposed to be about.

Her unfinished novel, *All the Dark and Beautiful Warriors,*[12] has not been published, but it was excerpted in 1983. The depth of her perceptions about women and men, their roles in society (Black and white), and the love with which she communicates this understanding are undeniable. The issues of class, sexism, and racism are addressed more adroitly in a few paragraphs of this unfinished work than in most of the volumes produced by the protests of the 1960s Black Nationalist Movement, much of whose literature rarely even acknowledges such issues.

There are several aspects to the tragedy of the loss of Lorraine Hansberry. When she died of cancer in 1965 she was not only a young woman (thirty-four), but a young writer. Her talent, her style, her ideas were being shaped by her emerging political consciousness. She was a young warrior in this "most expansive of revolutions."

She acknowledged that there is a unified system of thought that allows little Black girls to be blown to bits in Birmingham; that allows the flesh of Jews to be turned into lampshades; that allows generations of an indigenous people to be decimated in a place called the land of the free. It is the same system of thinking that allows women who have been raped to be treated as culpable, to have to justify their anger; that allows Dan White, who's killed a public official—Jewish and gay—to do less time in prison than if he'd robbed a bank.

Hansberry had considered this system of thought and taken a solid position. She would have been invaluable in the great divisive debate about whether or not Black women need feminism. In *Ebony* magazine in 1963 she wrote:

> *It is indeed a single march, a unified destiny and the prize is the future. In the ascent we shall want and need to lose some of the features of our collective personality for which we are justly ill-famed; but it is also to be hoped that we shall cling just as desperately to certain others for which we are not less harshly criticized. For above all, in behalf of an ailing world which sorely needs our defiance, may we as Negroes or women never accept the notion of "our place."*[13]

As a Black woman, writer, and lesbian-feminist, I need Lorraine Hansberry so that her brilliant vision illuminates my path. By leaving us her notebooks and fragments of work she has created an invaluable wealth of energy and resources for me as I search for the tradition of Black women writers and thinkers into which I properly fit.

In 1972 I taught at the Loft Film and Theater Center in a wealthy suburban town north of New York City. It was a very white, well-manicured, narrow little town. The Loft's goal was to have the privileged kids create art in cooperation with the working-class Black and Puerto Rican kids of the neighboring town. We were a hotbed of revolution to some parents and school officials. For the dozens of high school-age students the Loft was relief from the tedium of traditional education. In teaching my theatre class and putting on plays with the students I hoped to provide a place where they would find the intellectual independence and sense of mutual connection Hansberry had taught me to hold dear.

Etched on the marble stone of Hansberry's grave are these words from her play, *The Sign in Sidney Brustein's Window:*

> *I care. I care about it all. It takes too much energy not to care. . .The why of why we are here is an intrigue for adolescents; the how is what must command the living. Which is why I have lately become an insurgent again.*[14]

She has lately become an insurgent again, inside of me. I felt her moving me to action as I prepared this work. But she predicted that too. She knew that people/women would study the specifics of her life and find the universal truths we needed and we would claim her. In her last days she dictated her feelings and ideas into a tape recorder. At the end, she said:

> *If anything should happen—before 'tis done— may I trust that all commas and periods will be placed and someone will complete my thoughts—This last should be the least difficult— since there are so many who think as I do. . .*[15]

She was right, again.

NOTES

1. From a speech delivered at a Black writers' conference in 1959. Cited in *To Be Young, Gifted, and Black,* adapted by Robert Nemiroff (New York: New American Library, 1969), 41.

2. Barbara Smith, "Toward a Black Feminist Criticism," *Conditions: Two* (October 1977) 42-47.

3. Loften Mitchell, *Black Drama* (New York: Hawthorne Books, 1967), 49.

4. Langston Hughes, "Montage of a Dream Deferred," in *Selected Poems/Langston Hughes* (New York: Vintage Books, 1974), 268.

5. Lorraine Hansberry, *A Raisin in the Sun* (New York: New American Library of World Literature, 1959), 11-12.

6. Jonathan Katz, *Gay American History* (New York: Thomas Y. Crowell, 1976), 425.

7. Adrienne Rich, "The Problem with Lorraine Hansberry," *Freedomways*, Vol. 19, No. 4 (1979), 253.

8. Ibid., 50.

9. Lorraine Hansberry's unpublished, untitled notes, New York City, November 16, 1955. As quoted in Margaret Wilkerson, "Lorraine Hansberry: The Complete Feminist," *Freedomways*, Vol. 19, No. 4 (1979), 244.

10. Lorraine Hansberry, "Village Intellect Revealed," *New York Times*, October 31, 1964, Section 2, 3.

11. Lorraine Hansberry, "On Summer," *Playbill*, June 27, 1960, 27.

12. Lorraine Hansberry, *All the Dark and Beautiful Warriors*, unpublished. Excerpted in the *Village Voice*, August 16, 1983, with introduction by Thulani Davis.

13. Lorraine Hansberry, "This Complex of Womanhood," *Ebony* (September 1963).

14. Lorraine Hansberry, *The Sign in Sidney Brustein's Window*, quoted in the preface to Anne Cheney, *Lorraine Hansberry* (Boston: Twayne Publishers, 1984).

15. *To Be Young, Gifted, and Black*, adapted by Robert Nemiroff (New York: New American Library, 1969), 265.

BECAUSE SILENCE IS COSTLY

Nana and me (1982)
Photo: Ann Chapman

I have come to believe over and over again that what is most important to me must be spoken, made verbal and shared, even at the risk of having it bruised or misunderstood. That the speaking profits me; beyond any other effect.

Audre Lorde[1]

To speak of who we are as African-Americans has traditionally been a sign of triumph over adverse conditions. It was the telling of how we rose "up from slavery" into freedom and independence. It was a tale told in the early narratives of former slaves collected while other Black women and men were still held in bondage in this country. And in letters, magazine articles, and autobiographies written by African-Americans during the past two centuries. This tale of survival was and still is told around the kitchen tables of Black Americans in banter, jokes, in song and legend. And most exquisitely, it is written in the fiction that Black women and men have been creating almost as long as we have been sharing our oral histories.

To speak of who we are as Black lesbians and gays is equally as urgent and as triumphant a story, one whose telling has been somewhat more guarded. To say you are a lesbian or gay man to your family, friends, or co-workers is made difficult by a number of factors that have raised coming out (that process of speaking who we are) from a simple declaration into an important rite of passage. The psychological, social, and biblical misinformation dominating heterosexual assessment of lesbian/gay life makes coming out a nightmare for many of us, regardless of ethnicity. My own was unusually rewarding: my family responded as thinking, loving people, not as heterosexuals gripped by fear. The only pain was in the years before I was actually able to speak the words aloud. But other reactions vary—threats of (and actual) institutionalization, physical violence, ostracizing one's partner, rejection from the family. And because of a presumption of heterosexuality in this society, coming out is a process which must be repeated over and over again.

In the telling of our lives as African-Americans, being lesbian or gay was not something to "speak on." It did not fit the social picture of normality African-Americans wished to project in order to combat racist stereotypes. Nor did it suit the political strategies outlined by church and civil rights leaders for liberation.

Nevertheless, an individual's need to come out of the closet and name her/himself sexually is not only part of a political strategy but is, more fundamentally, at the core of accepting adulthood and validating one's own experience. Coming out is not merely announcing a personal choice to the world; it is a step in accepting your identity. For Black lesbians/gays it means saying both *I am gay* and also declaring *I am still Black*.

The coming-out story has acted as a major unifying thread in a lesbian/gay community that is as diverse as the United States itself. At any women's bar, or lesbian caucus, or lesbian and gay film festival, the participants represent a cross section of America, embracing divergent class, political, and ethnic identities. This diversity, which has been an important part of the strength of the Movement, also makes it difficult to maintain coalitions. A reinterpretation of the traditional coming-of-age story, the coming-out story has been the one bond that touches all. Everyone, whether already out or deeply closeted, is able to discuss the experience of sharing their life choice. It becomes a linguistic currency that allows all lesbians and gays at least one place in which they can identify with each other. As such, it also places Black lesbians and gays in conflict with Black culture where it is considered a risk to the entire community to say such things aloud.

The coming-out story occupies an important place in African-American letters for several reasons. First, its genesis in a political movement, as well as its frequent practice by non-writers and professional writers alike, are significant literary factors, much as they were when slave narratives were being collected, or during the Black Arts Movement of the 1960s. Second, and perhaps most interesting, is the close relationship the coming-out story has to the pure oral tradition of African-Americans and the slave narratives of the nineteenth and early twentieth centuries. It preserves the natural speech patterns of the one who is telling the story, and is usually a tale of triumph over repressive conditions in which the narrator emerges with a stronger, more positive identity. The emphasis in coming-out stories is, as is often true in autobiographies and slave narratives, on the importance of the story itself rather than the literary form in which the story is conveyed. It captures the irony, wit, and wisdom frequently exhibited in traditional African-American storytelling. And it is through the interview or oral narrative that the stories of those who do not consider themselves writers are best recorded, giving a truer reflection of the breadth of the Black lesbian and gay community.

The Black coming-out story continues to evolve in a variety of forms. The overriding theme and focus of these stories is a reconciliation of gay lifestyles with Black identity, a regaining of a sense of wholeness within oneself and with one's Black community. But any move toward this reconciliation must always confront the peculiar position the Black community has historically held regarding sex. In her article, "The Failure to Transform: Homophobia in the Black Community," Cheryl Clarke points out:

> We have expended much energy trying to debunk the racist mythology which says our [Black] sexuality is depraved. Unfortunately, many of us have overcompensated and assimilated the Puritan value that sex is procreation, occurs only between men and women, and is only valid within the confines of heterosexual marriage.[2]

The growth of the Women's Movement, following on the energy of the Civil Rights Movement in the '60s and in tandem with the Anti-War Movement of the '70s, provided a crucial opportunity for Black women to explore their lives, history, and art. Despite the repressive attitude toward public discussion of sex and gender in this country, such movements inevitably led to the exploration of sexuality and heterosexual roles for both women and men. Before "outing" became a political tool and a way to sell magazines, activists extolled the virtues of coming out as a serious political and personal action. But outing was always a tactic favored in some quarters.

Such was the case with civil rights leader Bayard Rustin as he organized the historic 1963 March on Washington. Speaking in a newspaper interview in 1987, Rustin recalled:

> *Then Strom Thurmond stood in the Senate speaking for three-quarters of an hour on the fact that Bayard Rustin was a homosexual, a draft dodger and a communist. Newspapers all over the country came out with this front page story. Mr. [A. Phillip] Randolph waited for the phone to ring. And it did indeed ring.*[3]

Rustin indicates in that article and others that his sexual orientation was always known among the political leaders with whom he worked, including Mr. Randolph, Martin Luther King, Jr., and Roy Wilkins. In 1960 Rustin had agreed to step down as an advisor to Dr. King when it was suggested his participation might jeopardize any effort King led. Rustin was nevertheless charged with organizing the 1963 march. He indicates that the accusations of homosexuality were lost, a response Thurmond could not have anticipated, among those of draft evasion (Rustin, a Quaker, had spent three years in prison as a conscientious objector) and communism (he had been a socialist). Although Rustin received support from both Randolph and King, his public presence diminished greatly after the Strom Thurmond attack. Before his death in 1987 Rustin worked quietly with the A. Phillip Randolph Educational Fund and contributed his support to gay organizations such as Men of All Colors Together and the National Coalition of Black Lesbians and Gays. His sentiments on coming out were unequivocal: "Every Gay who is in the closet is ultimately a threat to the freedom of Gays. . . Remaining in the closet is the other side of prejudice against Gays."[4]

On the other hand, for renowned blues singer Alberta Hunter the idea of coming out publicly as a lesbian was unthinkable. The distinct difference between her feelings and those of Bayard Rustin may, in part, be explained by their age difference (she was probably more than ten years his senior). But upbringing was certainly an important factor.

The strongest impulses that Hunter, also a songwriter, with material recorded by singers such as Bessie Smith, appears to have followed throughout her life and career were establishing financial security and promoting an air of personal propriety. A friend, Harry Watkins, recalls that Hunter "even had Confederate dollars. That's how much she saved money!"[5] And Hunter certainly learned strict lessons at home about modesty. She recalls that when growing up in Memphis she was not allowed to go barefoot even inside her house. Her sense of privacy, which was certainly a by-product of such upbringing, was reinforced by some of her friends. Watkins, being interviewed for Hunter's biography after her death, when questioned about her long-lasting affair with Lottie Tyler, refused to comment: "He rolled his eyes and sang a few lines of 'T'ain't Nobody's Business If I Do.' "[6]

Despite her growing popularity in the U.S. and Europe, Hunter guarded her personal relationships with women with a tenacity most others, like comedian Jackie Moms Mabley, refused to bother with. A ladylike presence was imperative to the persona Hunter created on the stage and to her own sense of self. In her biography she expresses her reluctance to sing on the infamous Beale Street in New Orleans. This attitude helped to isolate Hunter within the context of her relationships from a community of women who were less closeted than she. According to her biographers, "Alberta was a lesbian . . . but did everything to conceal this preference all her life. In her mind lesbianism tarnished the image of propriety and respectability she struggled so hard to achieve."[7] No doubt the perceived threat of losing her audience was a major factor in her concern about exposure. Ironically, by the time Hunter made her triumphant comeback in the 1970s, her lesbianism was legend and drew an entirely new audience of young women who came to see a part of lesbian history, sitting side by side with those who remembered her from her earlier career.

> . . . in the open fact of our loving
> with not only our enemies' hands
> raised against us
> means a gradual sacrifice
> of all that is simple
> dreams. . .
>
> Audre Lorde[8]

One of the first Black lesbians to freely identify herself as such is Anita Cornwell, who published fiction and articles in *The Ladder*, the lesbian journal originally produced by the Daughters of Bilitis. The publication amazingly survived the McCarthy era. Episodes in Cornwell's coming-out story are collected in her book, *Black Lesbian in White America*. The six chapters written in the third person relate Cornwell's initially secret relationship with her first woman lover, Zelmar, who seems to straddle both the lesbian and straight worlds. At the start, Cornwell's only connection with women in a lesbian context is her relationship with Zelmar, but she is aware of the gap already opening between her and her past life:

> *Emotionally, she [Anita] was still trapped within the wall she had erected around herself long ago when she was unable to fully cope with her environment in any other fashion . . . Although her friends were probably unaware of it, Anita was slowly edging away from them. Since the Gay world was unknown to her, however, she was moving into limbo.[9]*

While the relationship with Zelmar opens Cornwell to other relationships with women it is not until much later that she locates a women's community which gives her a certainty of identity and the promise of a fulfilling life as a lesbian.

When Cornwell began writing this material (1972) Ann Allen Shockley's novel, *Loving Her,* the first explicit and sympathetic book about a Black lesbian, was still two years in the future. In that light, Cornwell remains the first visible Black lesbian activist, and her work is designed as a documentation— much as the slave narratives recorded in the early twentieth century were.

Another coming-out story that is also essentially a documentation is that of Mabel Hampton which appeared in the *Lesbian Herstory Archives Newsletter.* It is a transcribed oral presentation, including a question-and-answer segment done by Hampton who was born in 1902. Its charm lies in its immediacy and Hampton's sparkling personality. The beginning is a long narrative describing her running away from home at an early age and being raised in Jersey City, New Jersey. It blossoms, though, when Hampton describes her life as a dancer, and meeting Lillian, who was to become her life partner for over forty years.

> *In 1932 I was on Lexington Avenue waiting for the streetcar. There were streetcars in those days and*

a girl says "Are you going. . ." She was just my
height. She said "Are you going uptown?" I said
"Yes." She said "You gonna catch the car?" I said
"I'm gonna catch the streetcar." So she says "All
right I'm going to too." I looked her up and down
and said to myself goodness gracious this is a good
looking chick. I said I wonder if she's in my life be-
cause you see I had danced on the stage and knew
all the answers.[10]

The final part of the story is in the form of questions and answers in which specific inquiries are made about nightspots the women who were "in the life" (lesbians) visited and other elements of Hampton's social life. When asked how old she was when she came out Hampton responds: "Well, I must have come out when I was eight years old. To tell the truth I never was in so I must have been out."[11]

The oral form captures Hampton's turn of phrase, sense of humor, and playfulness, and with it more of the essence of the Harlem Renaissance and the Depression eras. It also gives insight into the postwar period when Hampton had retired from the stage and worked as a cleaning woman in New York City. Her particularly inclusive manner of narrating, capturing colloquialisms of the period and providing physical details, gives her story a very broad perspective.

Leave my eyes   alone
why should I make
believe this place entirely
is white
and I am nothing. . .
                    June Jordan[12]

In 1979, the same year I came out to my mother and grandmother in a Times Square movie theater, *Essence* magazine published the coming-out story of Chirlane McCray:

> *When I decided to write this article, I said, "I'm writing this for my gay sisters..." As I wrote and relived the pain, I realized that the fears, which I had assumed to be gone, were still within me...I worry that no employer will hire me again, that my free-lance writing assignments will dwindle, that my gay friends who are still in the closet will disassociate themselves from me. I fear, in sum, that the monster of conformity will rear its angry head and devour me.*[13]

Her father's response, "You're Black and you're a woman ...I don't see why you want to be involved in something like this,"[14] echoes a common attitude among some in the Black community. The fallacy that homosexuality is "white" has been used frequently to try to shame Black gays into "recanting."

Neither of McCray's parents was wholly approving, but she was not met with hatred or reprisals. This reaction certainly played a part in enabling her to publish her coming-out story under her own name in a national magazine. Her purpose—to offer an example to those living in isolation—could not have been better fulfilled than by writing in a glossy, fashion magazine marketed to the mainstream population of Black women, many of whom might never have the courage to look for a lesbian community.

Essence had, in an earlier (June 1978) issue, published an interview with Lea Hopkins, who was identified as the first Black *Playboy* bunny, from Kansas City, Missouri. At the time of the interview Hopkins was no longer working as a bunny or a model, but was active in the Missouri lesbian political community. The interview was, unlike a coming-out story, a glossy magazine profile. It avoided any lengthy discussion of emotional or political issues. Although the piece was not sensationalistic, the focus was on Lea Hopkins as a startling phenomenon rather than the impact of her personal journey. Her lesbianism could well have been skydiving, yak farming, or any hobby Blacks don't "usually" do. McCray's first-person account assumes the social and political importance of her information and disallows any shock value her discussion might have.

In 1991, *Essence* magazine published another coming-out story, this one written by *Essence* editor Linda Villarosa and her mother, Clara Villarosa, a bookseller.[15] Using alternating narratives between daughter and mother each expresses their expectations and disappointments with the roles they've been assigned. With the emphasis this time on the mother's coming to terms with her daughter's orientation, it is almost Clara Villarosa's coming-out story as much as it is Linda's. The article acknowledges that coming out is a growing-up process, and that in order for it to work both the lesbian or gay child and her/his parents and friends must share in the experience. The Villarosa coming-out story more clearly places the lesbian experience within the context of a Black family. Both daughter and mother explored what the process was of coming to terms with their identities (lesbian and mother of a lesbian) more easily within that realm, a perspective offered by few coming-out stories. It is a coming out made possible only by the hundreds of others that came before it.

Long before I could mention the hallow words
they heard and accepted with silent disfigured
   glances
But I realized I could no longer dance here in my
   old
hometown.

Salih Michael Fisher[16]

The Women's Movement and the articulation of the ideals of feminism helped to open the door to an appreciation by women of their own circumstances and a recognition of the qualities unique and valuable in being a woman. There was little parallel development for African-American men during the early 1970s. Response to the changing role of women in society and the increased publication of writing by Black women was frequently reactionary, even among those who'd been in the avant garde of the Black Arts Movement. In a 1977 interview Ishmael Reed commented on the low sales of his newest novel:

> *...but the book only sold 8000 copies. I don't*
> *mind giving out the figure: 8000. Maybe if I was*
> *one of those young female Afro-American writers*
> *that are so hot now, I'd sell more. You know, fill*
> *my books with ghetto women who can do no*
> *wrong...But come on..."*[17]

Although men like Amiri Baraka and Henry Louis Gates have edited anthologies of writing by women since that time there has not been a real brotherly welcome of Black women's newfound voices.

In the mid-1980s Black gay men began to develop organizations with social and political activities that encouraged the type of publication women of color had been enjoying. Groups such as Black and White Men Together (later, Men of All Colors Together—nationally—and the Blackheart Collective—in New York City—began to form and acknowledge the role of sexual politics in the Black community, identifying the connection between sexism and homophobia. This also marked the first time that Black men made a visible, united commitment to any movement other than Civil Rights or Black Power.

A number of factors can be identified that contributed to the rise in gay male, and specifically Black gay male, activism. Repressive political measures initiated by federal and local governments have been more pronounced in the past fifteen years (the so-called Family Protection Act is one example) and increasingly reactionary court rulings, such as that in the case of *Bowers* v. *Hartwick* have occurred. But the most dramatic factor in the growth of an activist spirit and support of political organizations by African-American men is, of course, the outbreak of AIDS. In addition to AIDS work, such as fundraising, establishing personalized health support systems, and legal aid, the renewed impetus to organizing led to a burst of artistic growth. Like early lesbian activists, Black gay men developed a political consciousness about being gay and concurrently began to feel the importance of exploring their Black identities and documenting their lives for future generations.

One example of that expanded field of activism and documentation is *In the Life*.[18] The first collection of its kind, this anthology of poetry, essays, interviews, and short stories by Black gay men was edited by Joseph Beam. Part of its significance is the public stature of some of the Black gay men included in the publication. There is additional material about Bayard Rustin along with interviews with California singer, Blackberri, Harlem Renaissance writer, Bruce Nugent, and science fiction writer, Samuel R. Delaney, each of whom speaks of a type of dislocation from the larger society which facilitated being open.

In another anthology, *Black Men/White Men,* the story of Ron Vernon describes the conditions that surrounded his coming out. They reflect a similar type of alienation, though more extreme, than that expressed in the stories of Blackberri, Nugent, or Delaney. Vernon says:

> *When I was ten or eleven I began to get into a couple of arguments, deep arguments... At about thirteen, I transferred to a high school which was one of the roughest high schools in Chicago. Not knowing I would be the only overt homosexual at the school, the first day I wore a red shirt down to my knees and a pair of the loudest pants I could find.*[19]

Ron Vernon's coming out was met by violence dictated in part by the socioeconomic conditions of his life in Chicago in the 1960s, conditions that are a sharp contrast to the middle-class gentility of other times and families. The prevalence of bloody gang war activity set a deadly tone for anyone giving voice to individuality, much less gayness. Conflicts with students led to fights and eventually to incarceration, in both mental and penal institutions. He says of his stay in one such facility:

> *Whenever a prisoner called me a faggot or a punk, I would try to knock their brains out and shit like that. They thought they knew so much about psychology and about homosexuality that they could just put us in any type of situation and we would just play along with whatever was the set rules.*[20]

Vernon's insistence on staying out as a gay man, even under the most difficult and dangerous circumstances, led him to an expanded consciousness in many areas, including the relationship of gay pride to feminism. He says:

*. . .we have to really deal with sexism, and that's
really a strange thing to talk about—that you're
oppressed in a sexist sort of way, and that you
have to raise your own consciousness on sexism.
But I can see it, because Black people are consistently raising their own consciousness about their
Blackness, and so that's how I relate to it.*[21]

The 1980s saw the publication of the first full-length
coming-out stories by Black writers—Audre Lorde's *Zami: A New
Spelling of My Name* (1982) and Larry Duplechan's *Blackbird*
(1986)—in which a broader range of issues are addressed. Each
offers that important perspective of speaking from both inside
and outside a Black community in a distinctive voice. The stories occur in different time periods and different parts of the
U.S., but each testifies in a similar way to the endurance of Black
consciousness and the ability to integrate the many aspects of
one's personality and create a whole person.

Blackbird is, according to its publisher, a fiction. Yet it is
also described as a coming-out story and, as such, is the first
published book by a Black man in this genre. The narrator is
Johnnie Ray Rousseau (named for the singer popular in the
1950s), who lives with his parents in California in the mid-1970s
and attends a predominantly white high school. Although he
is active in dramatic productions and popular, he suffers feelings of isolation. Because Johnnie Ray acknowledges his role
as the "different one" (he is Black), his homosexuality does not
have a strong negative impact on him. His gayness becomes
a precious characteristic he keeps private. It, like being Black
in a white world, cannot be fully appreciated by those around
him.

From the opening comic line it is clear that the perspective is that of an erudite youth who has not found the appropri-

ate path to his true identity but will no doubt do so.

> *I dreamed I was dancing the waltz with Sal
> Mineo. He was young, about the age when he did*
> Crime in the Streets *which is about my age now*
> . . . . *I remember feeling awkward, my feet unsure
> of which way to go* . . . *And Sal Mineo said, "Don't
> worry; just follow me."*
> *I woke up suddenly as if awakened by a loud
> noise. My underpants were wet and sticky. And
> it was time to get up for school.*[22]

His devotion to theatre provides a direction in Johnnie's life, but it also delivers his first dose of sickening reality. When he tries out for the lead in the school play, *Hooray for Love,* Johnnie Ray is certain he will not be chosen. The play is about couples, and it is unlikely the drama instructor will risk casting the gangly Black youth opposite a young white girl in a musical that is essentially about romance and happy endings. But his audition is a success with the other students who are also auditioning, so hope slips in under the wall of defense that Johnnie has erected. When the cast list is posted, however, Johnnie is not on it. Instead he has been enlisted as "student director," the conciliatory gesture he'd expected from the start. But the certainty of how good he'd been on stage leaves him vulnerable. Out of his hurt comes the courage to confront the director with his prejudice, an act that is Johnnie Ray's first coming out: as a Black person who will not be silent about racism.

Throughout his experiences Johnnie Ray shows serious concern for how things affect his friends as well as himself. He maintains a loving relationship with the high school girl with whom he experiments sexually, although they both accept that their experimentation has only confirmed Johnnie's homosexuality. When confronted with his parents' disapproval of his gayness he is uncertain what to expect:

> *Not that it would have occurred to me to fear ac-*
> *tual bodily harm from the very people who gave*
> *me life. On the other hand neither was I so naive*
> *as to suppose I could simply march up to Mom*
> *(standing by the stove stirring roux gravy and*
> *singing "In the Sweet-By-and-By" softly to her-*
> *self) and say, "Excuse me, Mom, but I just wanted*
> *you to know I'm a homosexual," and expect her*
> *to say, "That's fine, baby; dinner be ready soon."*[23]

He has already learned that bodily harm is certainly one of the possibilities. A fellow student has been hospitalized after being beaten brutally by his father when the son's homosexuality was discovered. But in Johnnie's case the beating is psychological, and it is the sensation of being both actor and audience that sees Johnnie through the ordeal.

When Johnnie's parents are informed of his homosexuality they immediately confront him with such fear and ignorance that it is impossible for there to be any discussion. Johnnie responds:

> *I didn't want my own parents wishing I'd*
> *never been born, didn't want them to hurt and cry*
> *and think me sick and godless (and tell me so to*
> *my face). I couldn't help thinking perhaps it might*
> *be better to have your father break your face and*
> *get it over with, though I couldn't say I exactly*
> *wanted that either.*
> *But did I want to be normal?*[24]

What happens is more than Johnnie Ray could have expected. The family minister suggests that he is in the possession of "unclean spirits."

"What?" Mom, Dad and I said in chorus.
"You're saying I'm possessed? Like in The Ex-
orcist*?"*
"In a manner of speaking."[25]

When Johnnie submits to a rigorous prayer session, designed to relieve him of the suspected spirits, he assumes the
posture of prayer to mollify his parents but disassociates himself psychologically from the proceedings. Observing his family
and the specialist who's been brought in "petitioning the Al-
mighty with all their collective might,"[26] Johnnie decides:

If it hadn't been me down there on Solomon
Hunt's living room floor, I might have found a cer-
tain dark humor in the situation. But it was me.
And it wasn't funny. I felt sad and cold, and very
much alone. And I knew what I had to do.
I screamed.[27]

He accommodates his parents by faking his conversion,
being "saved." The real end of the story occurs in an epilogue.
Johnnie, a U.C.L.A. student, describes the first meeting of the
Gay Students' Union. "That meeting was like the world's big-
gest homecoming for me. . ." and the final line of the book,
"You couldn't slap this smile off my face."[28]

Duplechan's work offers an important opportunity to expand what it means to be an African-American. The perspective of a young Black man growing up in southern California
during the 1970s is certainly an important addition to the bi-
ographical tradition which rarely explores in depth the adolescent years of its subjects. That the young man has a gay identity makes his perspective—within the community and outside
of it—even more valuable. He is ultimately seeking a vision of
life that includes more than his parents or their minister would

have allowed. He will not relinquish an important aspect of his personality simply to make someone else feel more comfortable. The act of coming out, revealing the full range of his personality, is an impassioned plea for acceptance, but also a simple declaration that makes leaving home inevitable.

As a work of literature *Blackbird* is enhanced by the quirky, camp, gay male humor one would expect from a piece depicting the 1970s. This element is a wonderful entrée into that world, providing us with the tone that dominated a good bit of gay male life during that decade. Yet the author, and this may be due in part to the book's identification as a fiction, pulls back too often, providing humor when we want to know more about the narrator's feelings. Unlike a taped oral history, or even an interview, we cannot catch any turn of phrase or sentiment the author and editor do not wish to explore.

It is definitely valuable, however, to look at what Duplechan is able to do with a fictional form to expand our knowledge of Black life and Black gay adolescence. The use of humor is powerful in examining difficult topics. Here it evokes not only gay sensibilities but also traditional African-American humor, as well as providing a backbone or framework for what has all the essential earmarks of a family tragedy. Indeed, some tragic things do occur: a fellow student is viciously beaten by his father who discovers his homosexuality and another (a fellow on whom Johnnie Ray has had a long-standing crush) kills himself after his girlfriend dies during an illegal abortion. The humor allows us to believe in Johnnie Ray, though, and is what makes this story finally hold together. Duplechan's utilization of the African-American and the gay traditions of ironic humor rings as true for him in this work as it does for Mabel Hampton when she conveys the snappy wit of the Harlem Renaissance.

If it is wit that marks Larry Duplechan's work, it is the

poetic spirit and a strong political perspective that illuminates Audre Lorde's *Zami: A New Spelling of My Name*. Born in 1934, Lorde enjoyed an extensive career during the Civil Rights and Black Arts Movements in the 1960s and the Women's Movement in the 1970s. When *Zami* was published in 1982 it was described by the author as a "biomythography," a form combining elements of history, autobiography, and myth.

Lorde's choice to emphasize the scope of this autobiography is fortunate, for her book offers the first attempt at a full cultural and political exploration of what it means to be Black and gay in our society, and to be public about that identity. She begins with her childhood as the daughter of immigrant parents, carefully recreating the harsh reception her parents faced as alien Blacks in this country. Her descriptions of her own early jobs, particularly one in a Connecticut electronics factory, are clear lessons about what the political climate was for nonwhite and women workers in the 1950s:

> *Men ran the cutting machines. Most local people would not work under such conditions, so the cutting crew was composed of Puerto Ricans who were recruited in New York City. . . Nobody mentioned that carbon tet destroys the liver and causes cancer. . . Nobody mentioned that the X-ray machines, when used unsheilded, delivered doses of constant low radiation . . . Keystone Electronics hired Black women and didn't fire them after three weeks. We even got to join the union.*[29]

Her youthful experiences as a Black woman are a key to Lorde's acceptance of who she is and to her understanding of how people chose to lead their lives. She asks at the opening of the book:

> *To whom do I owe the power behind my voice,*
> *what strength I have become, yeasting up like sud-*
> *den blood from under the bruised skin's blister?*[30]

and she answers:

> *My father leaves his psychic print upon me, silent,*
> *intense, and unforgiving. But his is a distant light-*
> *ning. Images of women flaming like torches adorn*
> *and define the borders of my journey, stand like*
> *dykes between me and the chaos. It is the images*
> *of women, kind and cruel, that lead me home.*[31]

Her mother's vivid memories of and longing for her island home, Cariacou, are as much a part of Lorde's consciousness as the streets of Harlem. And it is to that place that Lorde turns when she affirms the interconnection between her roots as a Black woman and her life as a lesbian. The word *zami* origi- nated on one of the small islands that is part of Grenada—her mother, Linda's, birthplace: "Madivine. Friending. Zami. How Cariacou women loved each other is legend in Grenada, and so is their strength and beauty."[32] Throughout the book Lorde continues to draw on her experience growing up Black to help define herself as a lesbian.

One relationship Lorde has in her high school years seems outwardly typical of youthful bonding except that, in fact, it is a love that has no name yet. Lorde describes the hijinks she and her beloved Genevieve share in spite of the inhospitable attitude Lorde's parents have about visitors and her choice of acquaintances. Typically, their adverse response to the friend- ship is not effective at lessening the intense feeling between the girls. But in spite of the intimacy of their relationship, Genevieve still does not share with Audre the physical, possi- bly sexual, abuse she suffers from her stepfather.

This indignity and her inability, as a child, to perceive any alternative, leads Genevieve to suicide. Lorde then makes a list:

> *Things I never did with Genevieve: Let our bodies touch and tell the passions that we felt. Go to a Village gay bar, or any bar anywhere. Smoke reefer. Derail the freight that took circus animals to Florida. Take a course in international obscenities. Learn Swahili. See Martha Graham's dance troupe. Visit Pearl Primus. Ask her to take us away with her to Africa next time. Write THE BOOK. Make love.*[33]

In that youthful litany lies much of the spirit which fuels Lorde's life and work. She approaches each experience as if time may be limited so everything must be lived fully. Two weeks after her graduation from high school Audre leaves home to give further shape to her life. She makes a conscious decision to have a relationship with a woman, travel to Mexico, find a women's community, and maintain her own independence. These choices are so closely related that they seem one and the same. The description of each is well served by Lorde's highly sensuous use of language. The finely honed poetic imagery throughout the narrative does not preclude her addressing the reader directly, as if this were a taped narrative, like part of Mabel Hampton's coming-out story. When Lorde makes this break with the more immediate quality of the story it is generally to impart specific social history. She discusses, for example, the difficulty of finding a community of out Black lesbians in the 1950s. In sections like this we hear her voice, unadulterated, as if she's speaking into an oral historian's tape machine:

> *Most Black lesbians were closeted, correctly recog-*
> *nizing the Black community's lack of interest in*
> *our position. . .To be Black, female, gay and out of*
> *the closet in a white environment, even to the ex-*
> *tent of dancing in the Bagatelle, was considered by*
> *many Black lesbians to be simply suicidal.*[34]

But Lorde frequently conveys this type of concise cultural information within her dialogue. She describes two occasions which may typify the African-American community's reaction to lesbians. She says about her mother's response to a live-in lover at her Greenwich Village apartment:

> *My mother had met Muriel, and as usual since I*
> *left her house, knew it was wise to make no com-*
> *ment about my personal life. But my mother could*
> *make "no comment" more loudly and with more*
> *hostility than anyone else I knew.*[35]

Still her mother's anger is tied as much to Audre's daring to leave home as to living a lesbian life.

When Audre becomes involved in a relationship with Ginger, a co-worker in the Connecticut electronics factory, she begins to spend much of her time at Ginger's family's home. After a while Ginger's mother, Cora, addresses the fact of their relationship somewhat obliquely:

> *With her typical aplomb, Cora welcomed my in-*
> *creased presence around the house with the rough*
> *familiarity and browbeating humor due another*
> *one of her daughers. If she recognized sounds*
> *emanating from the sunporch on the nights I slept*
> *over, or our haggard eyes the next day, she ig-*
> *nored them. But she made it very clear that she*
> *expected Ginger to get married again. "Friends*

*are nice but marriage is marriage" she said to me
one night as she helped me make a skirt on her
machine. . . "And when she gets home don't be
thumping that bed all night, neither, because it's
late already and you girls have work tomorrow."*[36]

Lorde's ability to recreate the rhythms and idioms of Black speech along with the complex, even contradictory, set of ideas surrounding reaction to homosexuality make *Zami* important to the evolution of the coming-out story. In addition to introducing the political and social elements of Black gay life in a white world, Lorde, unlike most lesbian authors of coming-out stories, discusses her sexual life candidly. Her description of her affair with Ginger is innocent and enthusiastic, full of the sexual desire which at nineteen has been suppressed for too many years. Later, in Mexico, Audre is still emotionally inexperienced but enthusiastically expresses her desire for Eudora, the expatriot who is overcoming shame of her own body which has been scarred by a mastectomy:

*She rose slowly. I unbuttoned her shirt and she
shrugged it off her shoulders til it lay heaped at
our feet. In the circle of lamplight I looked from
her round firm breast with its rosy nipple erect
to her scarred chest. The pale keloids of radiation
burn lay in the hollow under her shoulder and
arm down across her ribs. I raised my eyes and
found hers again, speaking a tenderness my
mouth had no words for. . . My mouth finally
against hers, quick breathed, fragrant, searching,
her hand entwined my hair. My body took charge
from her flesh. Shifting slightly, Eudora reached
past my head toward the lamp above us. I caught*

her wrist . . ."No," I whispered against the hollow
of her ear. "In the light." [37]

In view of the difficulty the Black community has had with
the imagery assigned to our sexuality, as well as its ambivalence
about the role of those with nontraditional (i.e., not white
middle-class perceptions of) sexual lives, it is significant that
Lorde chooses to treat the sexual aspects of her narrative
openly. She refuses to equivocate in her coming-out story, never
attempting to either ignore her Blackness or to indicate that she
is a lesbian in spite of it. She also is able to acknowledge and
describe her political perspective on race, gender, and sexuality without relinquishing the specifics of her sexuality as a Black
woman and as a lesbian. Lorde's open exploration of the sexual nature of her life is an important departure from the
majority of writing by African-Americans, either fictional or autobiographical. *Zami* offers one of the first honest glimpses of
Black lesbian sexuality in American literature devoid of a need
to place blame or locate causality.

Lorde's celebration of the sexuality essential to her life, and
significant in lesbian and gay life generally, is an exciting step
in African-American literature. For many years, and certainly
in the recent past shadowed by AIDS, gays have often down-
played the role of sexuality in an effort to deflect criticism. In
addition, antipornography activists, representing in many cases
more repressive elements of feminism, have attempted to set
standards for the appropriate and inappropriate depiction of
sexuality. This has cast a pall over some members of the creative community who might consider exploring sex in their literary fiction or autobiographical material. Lorde's work is a coming out not only as a Black lesbian but also as a sexual being
whose goal is the successful integration of all of these elements
of her life.

In an article entitled "The Historical Text as Literary Artifact" Hayden White says, ". . . histories gain part of their explanatory effect by their success in making stories out of mere chronicles. . ."[38] Lorde strives to pull her story out of the realm of "mere chronicle" by defining it as a biomythography. She opens up the autobiography to include the political and historical perspectives she feels are crucial to the telling of her story as a Black lesbian. It also allows Lorde, the poet, to use the lyrical imagery that marks her other writing, imbuing her coming-out story with a mythical quality. Lorde's abilities as a poet and essayist provide her story with the best elements of direct oral history as well as those of historical fiction. With her good ear for dialogue, she captures the powerful turns of phrase which give events immediacy. She also utilizes the dramatic tension that enhances all storytelling, whether traditional or fictional. *Zami* is the most fully realized coming-out story that the gay and Black communities have. It offers a vision of what it means to be *other,* explores the overlapping issues faced by both groups, and makes clear the bonds that will forever bind anyone who is a member of both the gay and Black communities.

The appearance of two full-length works, Lorde's biomythography and Duplechan's fiction, signifies a shift in the perceived value of the coming-out story and its place in the literary canon of African-Americans. Until recently most coming-out stories were, like those of Hampton or Vernon, short pieces reproduced in anthologies. The presumption is that these longer works will appeal not only to those struggling with their own coming-out stories but also to a broad audience interested in history and autobiography and African-Americans.

Anthropologist John Langston Gwaltney, in preparing his book of twentieth-century narratives, *Drylongso,* found that "In black culture there is a durable, general tolerance, which is amazingly free of condescension, for the individual's right to follow the truth wherever it leads."[39] The important accomplishment of the books by Audre Lorde and Larry Duplechan is their success in following the truths of a Black lesbian/gay experience. And their unflinching portrayal of the Black community's varied response, even when it is shameful. Neither book sacrifices the exciting patterns of Black speech, the nuances of Black life in white America, the exploration of the African-American ambivalence about sexual imagery, or the complexity of gender relations in the Black community. Yet both maintain their integrity as gay stories. As narratives these books do what the Black coming-out story is intended to do: integrate racial and sexual identities in a way that creates a fully realized whole with potential for a positive impact.

In an article on the autobiographical writings of African-American women, Frances Smith Foster quotes historian Roy Harvey Pierce:

> When we come to try to understand our literature in our history and our history in our literature, . . .we have to be ready to see new forms, new modes, new styles emerging and to realize how all that is new results from a particular confrontation of [one] culture made by a particular [person] at a particular time."[40]

In coming-out stories it is first the revitalization of traditional forms—storytelling and narratives—that is most significant. Then it is the emergence of a new form—biomythography —which contributes to our understanding of our literature and our history. The validity of these forms in African-American culture reasserts itself in the new and the old voices which essentially tell stories of triumph from Black gays and lesbians.

Despite the effort of those in the Black community who have forsaken the tradition of "durable tolerance" that Gwaltney identified, banishing Black gays and lesbians from their homes or their literary forums, the coming-out story reaffirms the legitimacy of the role Black gays and lesbians continue to play in the Black community whether they are openly gay or not.

Many writers and editors in the fast-emerging commercial lesbian and gay community have exalted the development of lesbian/gay writing by saying it is no longer "just" coming-out stories. In some ways this is true. Lesbian and gay stories have many forms and always will. From Monique Wittig to Isabel Miller to Nikki Baker, from John Rechy to John Preston to Melvin Dixon to Assoto Saint, the stories take us many places in addition to out of the closet.

But the coming-out story may prove to be the most energetic and engaging aspect of the autobiographical form which is itself experiencing a resurgence in popularity. Biomythography is certainly an exciting genre for creative writers who wish to record their African-American sojourn within the language and emotional scope they've lived it. The blend of history, biography, and poetic spirit seems most suitable for Lorde's need to express both a strong political perspective as well as a highly charged personal account—a need that is familiar to many African-Americans who believe that "what is most important. . . must be spoken. . . ."

Black/Out,[41] the magazine published by the National Coalition of Black Lesbians and Gays, carried four stark words on the cover of one of its issues. They answered the question of why, in spite of fear, Black lesbians and gay men continue to write and speak their coming-out stories. The four simple words are the answer to the *why* of slave narratives and oral histories handed down to each generation. They tell us why coming-out stories find their niche so comfortably among the stories of all our forebears: *Because silence is costly.*

NOTES

1. Audre Lorde, "The Transformation of Silence into Language and Action," in *Sister Outsider* (Trumansburg, NY: The Crossing Press, 1984), 40.

2. Cheryl Clarke, "The Failure to Transform: Homophobia in the Black Community," in *Home Girls: A Black Feminist Anthology*, edited by Barbara Smith (Albany, NY: Kitchen Table: Women of Color Press, 1983), 199.

3. Bayard Rustin, interviewed in the *Village Voice*, June 30, 1987, 28.

4. Bayard Rustin, interviewed in *Black/Out*, Vol. 1, Nos. 3-4, 18.

5. Frank C. Taylor with Gerald Cook, *Alberta Hunter: A Celebration in Blues* (New York: McGraw-Hill, 1987), 72.

6. Ibid., 7.

7. Ibid., 43.

8. Audre Lorde, "Outlines," in *Our Dead Behind Us* (New York: W.W. Norton, 1986), 14.

9. Anita Cornwell, "Fleeing the Myths of Motherhood," in *Black Lesbian in White America*, (Tallahassee, FL: Naiad Press, 1983), 53.

10. Mabel Hampton, "Coming Out Story," *Lesbian Herstory Archives Newletter*, No. 7, (1981), 32.

11. Ibid., 33.

12. June Jordan, "And Who Are You?" in *Things I Do in the Dark* (Boston: Beacon Press, 1981), 98.

13. Chirlane McCray, "I Am A Lesbian," *Essence*, September 1979, 91.

14. Ibid., 161.

15. Linda Villarosa and Clara Villarosa, *Essence*, May 1991, 82, 126.

16. Salih Michael Fisher, "Assumption About the Harlem Brown Baby," in *Black Men/White Men*, edited by Michael J. Smith (San Francisco: Gay Sunshine Press, 1982), 31.

17. John Domini, "Roots and Racism: An Interview with Ishmael Reed, *Boston Phoenix*, April 5, 1977, 20.

18. *In the Life*, edited by Joe Beam (Boston: Alyson Publications, 1986).

19. Ron Vernon, "Growing Up in Chicago Black and Gay," in *Black Men/White Men*, 37.

20. Ibid., 42.

21. Ibid., 43.

22. Larry Duplechan, *Blackbird* (New York: St. Martin's Press, 1986), 1.

23. Ibid., 145-6.

24. Ibid., 153.

25. Ibid.

26. Ibid., 162.

27. Ibid.

28. Ibid., 182.

29. Audre Lorde, *Zami: A New Spelling of My Name* (Watertown, MA: Persephone Press, 1982), 126.

30. Ibid., 3.

31. Ibid.

32. Ibid., 14.

33. Ibid., 97.

34. Ibid., 224.

35. Ibid., 216.

36. Ibid., 114.

37. Ibid., 167-8.

38. Hayden White, "The Historical Text as Literary Artifact," in *Critical Theory Since 1965*, edited by Hazard Adams and Leroy Searles (Tallahassee: Florida State University Press, 1985), 397.

39. John Langston Gwaltney, *Drylongso* (New York: Random House, 1980), xxvii.

40. Roy Harvey Pierce, *Historicism Once More*, (Princeton, NJ: Princeton University Press, 1969), 59. Quoted by Frances Smith Foster, "Adding Color and Contour to Early American Self-Portraits," in *Conjuring*, edited by Marjorie Pryse and Hortense J. Spillers (Bloomington: Indiana University Press, 1985), 25.

41. Cover caption, *Black/Out*, Vol. 1, Nos. 3-4, 1987.

Other titles from Firebrand Books include:

Artemis In Echo Park, Poetry by Eloise Klein Healy/$8.95

Before Our Eyes, A Novel by Joan Alden/$8.95

Beneath My Heart, Poetry by Janice Gould/$8.95

The Big Mama Stories by Shay Youngblood/$8.95

The Black Back-Ups, Poetry by Kate Rushin/$8.95

A Burst Of Light, Essays by Audre Lorde/$8.95

Cecile, Stories by Ruthann Robson/$8.95

Crime Against Nature, Poetry by Minnie Bruce Pratt/$8.95

Diamonds Are A Dyke's Best Friend by Yvonne Zipter/$9.95

Dykes To Watch Out For, Cartoons by Alison Bechdel/$7.95

Dykes To Watch Out For: The Sequel, Cartoons by Alison Bechdel/$8.95

Exile In The Promised Land, A Memoir by Marcia Freedman/$8.95

Experimental Love, Poetry by Cheryl Clarke/$8.95

Eye Of A Hurricane, Stories by Ruthann Robson/$8.95

The Fires Of Bride, A Novel by Ellen Galford/$8.95

Food & Spirits, Stories by Beth Brant (*Degonwadonti*)/$8.95

Free Ride, A Novel by Marilyn Gayle/$9.95

A Gathering Of Spirit, A Collection by North American Indian Women edited by Beth Brant (*Degonwadonti*)/$10.95

Getting Home Alive by Aurora Levins Morales and Rosario Morales/$9.95

The Gilda Stories, A Novel by Jewelle Gomez/$9.95

Good Enough To Eat, A Novel by Lesléa Newman/$8.95

Humid Pitch, Narrative Poetry by Cheryl Clarke/$8.95

Jewish Women's Call For Peace edited by Rita Falbel, Irena Klepfisz, and Donna Nevel/$4.95

Jonestown & Other Madness, Poetry by Pat Parker/$7.95

Just Say Yes, A Novel by Judith McDaniel/$9.95

The Land Of Look Behind, Prose and Poetry by Michelle Cliff/$8.95

Legal Tender, A Mystery by Marion Foster/$9.95

Lesbian (Out)law, Survival Under the Rule of Law by Ruthann Robson/$9.95

A Letter To Harvey Milk, Short Stories by Lesléa Newman/$8.95

Letting In The Night, A Novel by Joan Lindau/$8.95

Living As A Lesbian, Poetry by Cheryl Clarke/$7.95

Metamorphosis, Reflections On Recovery by Judith McDaniel/$7.95

Mohawk Trail by Beth Brant (*Degonwadonti*)/$7.95

Moll Cutpurse, A Novel by Ellen Galford/$7.95

The Monarchs Are Flying, A Novel by Marion Foster/$8.95

More Dykes To Watch Out For, Cartoons by Alison Bechdel/$7.95

Movement In Black, Poetry by Pat Parker/$8.95

My Mama's Dead Squirrel, Lesbian Essays on Southern Culture by Mab Segrest/$9.95

New, Improved! Dykes To Watch Out For, Cartoons by Alison Bechdel/$7.95

The Other Sappho, A Novel by Ellen Frye/$8.95

Out In The World, International Lesbian Organizing by Shelley Anderson/$4.95

Politics Of The Heart, A Lesbian Parenting Anthology edited by Sandra Pollack and Jeanne Vaughn/$12.95

Presenting. . . Sister NoBlues by Hattie Gossett/$8.95

Rebellion, Essays 1980-1991 by Minnie Bruce Pratt/$10.95

Restoring The Color Of Roses by Barrie Jean Borich/$9.95

A Restricted Country by Joan Nestle/$9.95

Running Fiercely Toward A High Thin Sound, A Novel by Judith Katz/$9.95

Sacred Space by Geraldine Hatch Hanon/$9.95

Sanctuary, A Journey by Judith McDaniel/$7.95

Sans Souci, And Other Stories by Dionne Brand/$8.95

Scuttlebutt, A Novel by Jana Williams/$8.95

Shoulders, A Novel by Georgia Cotrell/$9.95

Simple Songs, Stories by Vickie Sears/$8.95

Spawn Of Dykes To Watch Out For, Cartoons by Alison Bechdel/$8.95

Speaking Dreams, Science Fiction by Severna Park/$9.95

Stone Butch Blues, A Novel by Leslie Feinberg/$10.95

The Sun Is Not Merciful, Short Stories by Anna Lee Walters/$8.95

Talking Indian, Reflections on Survival and Writing by Anna Lee Walters/$10.95

Tender Warriors, A Novel by Rachel Guido deVries/$8.95

This Is About Incest by Margaret Randall/$8.95

The Threshing Floor, Short Stories by Barbara Burford/$7.95

Trash, Stories by Dorothy Allison/$9.95

We Say We Love Each Other, Poetry by Minnie Bruce Pratt/$8.95

The Women Who Hate Me, Poetry by Dorothy Allison/$8.95

Words To The Wise, A Writer's Guide to Feminist and Lesbian Periodicals & Publishers by Andrea Fleck Clardy/$5.95

The Worry Girl, Stories from a Childhood by Andrea Freud Loewenstein/$8.95

Yours In Struggle, Three Feminist Perspectives on Anti-Semitism and Racism by Elly Bulkin, Minnie Bruce Pratt, and Barbara Smith/$8.95

You can buy Firebrand titles at your bookstore, or order them directly from the publisher (141 The Commons, Ithaca, New York 14850, 607-272-0000).

Please include $2.00 shipping for the first book and $.50 for each additional book.

A free catalog is available on request.